THE
SACRED VOW
A Memoir

Andrew Benzie Books
Martinez, California

Published by Andrew Benzie Books
www.andrewbenziebooks.com

Copyright © 2021 Yolanda Lopez
yolandalopezauthor@gmail.com

All rights reserved. Except as permitted under the U.S. Copyright Act of 1976, no part of this publication may be reproduced, distributed or transmitted in any form or by any means, or stored in a database or retrieval system without prior written permission of the author.

Printed in the United States of America
First Edition: February 2022

10 9 8 7 6 5 4 3 2 1

Lopez, Yolanda
The Sacred Vow

ISBN: 978-1-950562-39-8

Cover design by Ghislain Viau
www.creativepublishingdesign.com

Book design by Andrew Benzie
www.andrewbenziebooks.com

This book is dedicated to my daughter, Vanessa, in the hope she will now fully grasp my journey to love and motherhood and in doing so will understand what a treasured gift she has become.

*"Nothing is easier than self-deceit.
For what each man wishes that he also believes to be true."*
—Demosthenes, Third Olynthiac

Contents

Introduction 1
Chapter 1: The Lover 3
Chapter 2: The Interview 5
Chapter 3: Betrayal 7
Chapter 4: San Francisco 9
Chapter 5: Meeting an Irishman 15
Chapter 6: New Job Worries 19
Chapter 7: More Bad Bosses 23
Chapter 8: Meeting Albert 25
Chapter 9: Hospital Woes 27
Chapter 10: The Goodbye Party 31
Chapter 11: A New Love 35
Chapter 12: The Job Offer 43
Chapter 13: Albert Again 49
Chapter 14: School Days 51
Chapter 15: The Psychic's Prediction 59
Chapter 16: To Be or Not to Be 65
Chapter 17: The Dreaded Phone Call 71

Chapter 18: Yes or No 73

Chapter 19: The Agreement 77

Chapter 20: The Housing Dilemma 79

Chapter 21: Lamaze Worries 81

Chapter 22: Baby Qualms 83

Chapter 23: Panic at the Hospital 85

Chapter 24: Feeding Troubles 89

Chapter 25: Return to School and Vanessa's First Surgery 93

Chapter 26: Law School 97

Chapter 27: Shared Custody 103

Chapter 28: Bar Exam 107

Chapter 29: Raising Vanessa 109

Chapter 30: The Affair 111

Chapter 31: The Latter Years 117

Chapter 32: The Goodbye Letter 119

Chapter 33: The Later Years with Albert 123

Chapter 34: Final Reflections 127

Acknowledgements 129

INTRODUCTION

For thirty years, I have kept a careful secret I am now ready to reveal. This memoir is my attempt to sort out an early childhood decision that had made a lasting imprint on my life. I hope to finally understand the truths and falsehoods that were built on that youthful experience.

As I began writing it dawned on me that in order to share the most intimate parts of my life with the honor they deserved, I first had to do some serious reflection. My backwards look had to be without filters or self-deception. I had to determine if I had learned anything from the choices made as a young, inexperienced woman compared to the later ones made as a knowledgeable adult.

As many know, this type of soul-searching is not for the faint of heart because it is so easy to delude ourselves.

No one, except two close female friends, had had any knowledge of my secret. What no one else could have guessed was that I had an alternate existence with a secret lover. This memoir reveals that story and the discovery of a painful truth I made that had eluded me for most of my life.

Chapter 1
The Lover

As I glanced at my longtime lover, my eyes instinctively scanned the small Italian restaurant where we had met for so many intimate lunches and dinners, no longer worrying that people might recognize us. I watched as he absent-mindedly twirled his spaghetti around his fork, unaware of the marinara sauce drops splattering on his light blue chambray shirt.

How I had once loved this man! Our affair had gone on for thirty years, longer than most marriages, though not as long as the tenure of his marriage. But where had the time gone? His hair was now gray and sparse, not the dark, silver-streaked mane it had once been. He had difficulty walking and his eyesight and hearing were poor. His overall health was in general decline.

His death and authoring my story have taken me on an inward journey, forcing me to search deeper into the meaning of all the relationships that have touched me from my earliest days.

Sorting out what he and the others meant has pushed me to look more closely at what I thought I knew about love, who we love and why we love them. All along, I assumed I knew who the most important lover was—only to discover as I got into the writing that it may not have been so clear.

My personal belief is that we are here to love and be loved. This idea provoked an important question for me. Was it possible to love more than one person at a time, honestly and wholeheartedly? It is because I have done it. Love has ushered me into battlefields, disappointments, immense joy and to finally looking at betrayal directly in the face. It is only now in hindsight and with humility that

YOLANDA LOPEZ

I can look back at the highs and lows of my personal journey with gratitude and love for all that I have experienced and for those whom I have loved. Their love has inspired me and made me the loving and deeply flawed person I am today. For that I am forever thankful.

This is my story.

Chapter 2
The Interview

I remember the first time I met him. It seemed so long ago. He was interviewing me for a job I desperately needed after just finishing law school. As a single parent with a three-year-old daughter to support caring for her was my top priority, along with repaying student loans and finding housing. The interview went well. Both he and his assistant seemed happy with my responses. I was called back for a second interview.

That meeting was with him alone. He asked only one question. I knew instantly I should have answered it differently, but I couldn't help myself. I knew my response may have cost me the much-needed job. His question seemed simple and yet was so difficult: "If I give you specific directions to take an action you do not agree with, would you comply?"

Without hesitation, I declared, "No, I would try to get you to see another perspective."

"Okay," he said, surprised, "Would you comply when I made my request a second time?"

"No," I retorted. "I would continue trying to change your mind."

I knew this was the incorrect answer, but it slipped out of my mouth before I could revise an appropriate response in my head.

"When," he asked, clearly frustrated, "would you abide by my instructions?"

I wanted to say, "Never," but knew that's not what he wanted to hear. So, lowering my voice to take the edge off my reply, I said, "If I seriously didn't agree, I would continue trying to change your mind even after following your direction."

Leaving the interview, I shook my head in frustration, admonishing myself over and over. *I should not have been so candid! Why couldn't I just lie like others did in interviews? Why was it so hard for me?*

Despite my answer, he hired me. Many years later he confessed he thought I wasn't serious about never giving up on changing his mind when I did not agree. By then he had learned from hard experience I had told the truth. Laughingly and with loving affection, he would say he had never known anyone so persistent and determined to change someone's mind.

Chapter 3
Betrayal

From an early age, I received the message that you could not trust men. They would betray you.

Staggering out of the house that sweltering summer afternoon, I ran to the large palm tree in my front yard and sank down next to it. It had always been my safe place. Its trunk comforted my back like a cool hand as I slid closer to enjoy the shade from the palm tree's fronds. Tears spilled down my face as I lowered my head into my hands and sobbed. I was nine years old but felt much older. I didn't realize it fully then, but that day would have a profound influence on the rest of my life.

I couldn't believe what my mother had just told us. Our dad was leaving. We were moving to Los Angeles and would no longer be a family. I had seen how hard my parents had struggled and knew there were problems, but it had never occurred to me that my dad would desert us. I couldn't understand why he would leave us for another family. I thought he loved us.

Yes, I had heard my mother crying many nights in her room alone. I know she thought no one heard her, but it was impossible to ignore her muffled cries. Why would my dad do such a thing? I loved him so much and thought he was a good man. *But if good men could betray those they loved even though they professed to love them, and then leave them,* I thought to myself, *then surely none could be trusted.* Why would my dad leave his current family of five children to start a new one, especially with my mom pregnant with her sixth child? No, it wasn't right or fair.

So, in my ninth year under that special palm tree, I made a sacred vow to never marry or have children. I kept my solemn promise secret, simply telling my family and friends I would not be marrying or having children. They laughed, thinking those were the words of a child who would naturally grow up and change her mind.

It was my intention never to break that pledge, but I'll admit I did not keep all of my oath. Unforeseen circumstances, which touched me deeply, made me reconsider part of my promise. But I never changed my mind.

Chapter 4
San Francisco

As I sat in the crowded Los Angeles airport waiting patiently for the San Francisco boarding announcement, I felt the years of responsibility and caring for my siblings and my mother weighing heavily on my shoulders. The eldest of six children, I was often in charge and delegated to help my mother make decisions. I had never lived on my own. I needed to get away and start somewhere new. So, in 1967, at age 21, I was finally breaking free. It had been a hard decision.

I contemplated all that I was leaving—my family, my work, my friends—to start a new life in Northern California. I knew no one there, but I had a job and hopefully would meet new friends. I felt guilty, knowing I was deserting my mother, who was increasingly overwhelmed. But I felt I had no choice if I wanted to survive.

Though the airport was noisy, I thought I heard my name announced over the airport intercom system. Concentrating harder, I heard the announcer say there was a phone call waiting for me at the nearest white telephone. *Who would be calling me now and why?* Looking around for a white phone, I walked toward one and picked it up. The operator requested my name. "Just a moment," she said, "I'll put your call through."

It was my ex-boss, Jim, from Sun Life, the insurance company I had worked for in Los Angeles and the job I was leaving. "I couldn't let you leave without wishing you the best, Yolanda. You'll be missed. I was afraid I wouldn't get back in time to say goodbye," he said thoughtfully.

"Thank you, Jim. I am hoping for the best," I told him. My whole life was ahead of me. Jim's good wishes warmed my heart and brought back memories of my first and only job in Los Angeles. That insurance company was my initial exposure to the work environment. It was also where I learned the fine art of drinking.

Don, one of my favorite bosses, was always up for a beer or something stronger. A serious drinker, he frequently fell from his chair after returning to work from a hard-drinking lunch. His actual fall made a large thundering noise that could be heard throughout the office, because Don was quite pudgy. One of my tasks was to help him get back into his chair, but I couldn't do it alone. He weighed too much, so I had to ask for assistance from one of the stronger male employees. Nonetheless, Don was always grateful for the reseating and would laugh unabashedly.

I wore my long, dark hair in a French twist then and I suppose that, along with my stoic face, made me appear older than my actual age. Each evening after work we would all meet at the local nearby bar for a couple of drinks. I had been drinking at that pub for close to two years when the office group decided to celebrate my twenty-first birthday there. Out of friendliness the bartender asked me what birthday I was observing. He was dismayed to learn that I had been drinking there long before I was legal.

I would miss them all, including Norman, whom I'd had a secret crush on—well, not all that secret. Company policy forbade employees from dating. Jim was suspicious and had warned Norman after discovering some of my long, black hairpins on the floor of his Volkswagen. But that was in the past. I was moving on.

Jim had arranged for a transfer to one of Sun Life's offices in the Bay Area. My new boss, also coincidentally named Don, would pick me up and help me get settled in San Francisco. It was exciting and scary, but I was ready. In lots of ways, I had led a sheltered life and was not ready for some of the men I would encounter within the business world. Jim was protective of his female employees. I would soon discover that not all supervisors were like him. Some wanted to use their authority to force me into situations and relationships I did not want. I had not yet fully discovered the pitfalls of being young and naïve.

THE SACRED VOW

I spent my first night in San Francisco at Don's home with him and his wife. The next morning, I was served an English muffin, something I had not had before. San Francisco would be the beginning of my exposure to an array of new foods I had never seen, tasted or even knew existed. I grew to love raw oysters, artichokes, all types of fish and many other exciting foods that had never been on my plate in Los Angeles.

That morning my boss planned to show me several areas of San Francisco where I might want to live. He helped me locate a small studio apartment on Jefferson Street in the Marina District near the Palace of Fine Arts. It was a beautiful neighborhood with good transportation and a short walking distance to the San Francisco marina.

Initially, I had difficulty finding my apartment whenever I returned home because all the buildings in the Marina District were similar in size, color, and height. They had a distinctive look, and zoning requirements must have required certain colors because they were all the same colors. I often found myself lost, wandering around and trying to find my new home. I soon learned to pay attention only to the address.

It took me some time to get used to the new San Francisco sounds that were so unlike Los Angeles. The haunting reverberations of the nightly foghorns initially kept me awake. Eventually, they became part of the normal background noises and, when they were silent, I would awaken fearing something was amiss. I grew to love them. That, plus the hissing and clanging sounds echoing from the coiled steam heaters common in old San Francisco housing, required a new perspective on nighttime resonances. For the first few months I tossed and turned each evening until I learned to adjust to the new wails and clangs that came with my small studio apartment.

I loved being in San Francisco, particularly the climate. I had always visited in the Fall, so I was unfamiliar with the summer weather. My move to the Bay Area in May coincided with the beginning of the foggy season. I awoke each morning to foggy days, hoping for sunshine. When the sun deemed to peak out, it would be quickly overshadowed by the returning fog. Cloudy overcast weather lingered until early September when the beautiful sunny weather returned. I missed the hot Los Angeles sunshine and the long stretches of beaches. The San Francisco beaches were cold, windy, and often overcast, but I soon grew to appreciate this new type of beach.

I was astounded at the bright blue skies and the lack of smog. In the early years of my move to the Bay Area, I saw only fog and haze. In the later years, with an increased population, the haze would turn into smog; but it was still called "haze." When I tried to point out that smog had a distinctive yellow tinge, Northern Californian's would look at me weirdly, denying it was smog. Being a true Angeleno who grew up in the days of smog alerts, I knew smog when I saw it. Only recently, fifty years later, have some Bay Area weather reporters dared to allude to the haze by its rightful name, smog.

The year of my arrival, 1967, was also the "Summer of Love," with the Haight-Ashbury District as the center of all the activity. I would wander down there to observe the happenings and the external trappings of the hippie movement, including the music, the drugs, and the protests. But I remained an observer more than a participant. I liked the incense, not patchouli, and the flowers; but it was all too wild for the inhibited girl I was at that point. I was content to watch from the sidelines. I saw lots of begging, drugs and lost girls looking for love. I decided I would never be a tie-dye fan.

I remained very much an L.A. girl in dress, ideas, and philosophy. My differences stood out especially with my Berkeley friends. I soon learned that none of my new friends, at least the ones my age, wore makeup or were as concerned about their clothing as I was; nor did they believe in shaving their underarms or legs. I was stunned and didn't know how to respond. I continued in my "L.A. ways," which amused them.

My biggest revelation came when they invited me to their weekly evening hot tub outing. Albany Hot Tubs had large outdoor tubs that could be shared with up to six other people. I wasn't prepared for what happened when we arrived. There were no single dressing rooms. Although I knew everyone would be naked in the hot tubs, I didn't think we would have to undress in front of each other and then walk naked from the dressing room. I was shy and had never undressed in front of others, even females. None of this seemed to concern them. I tried to hide my embarrassment the first couple of times, but always felt awkward. I eventually felt more comfortable with the undressing part, but I never stopped shaving my legs or underarms.

When I moved to the Bay Area I was still a virgin. A reluctant one, but a fussy one. Old religious beliefs still lingered in my mind, but I was determined to change my status with the move. I kept thinking I was so old, and my inexperience needed to be remedied. I wasn't sure how since I knew no one and especially not any willing men when I first arrived. Well, there was my boss, but he was married, and I wasn't interested in him. He hinted he was available though he did not know my virgin status.

It was shortly after I had settled in San Francisco that I got a phone call from a former co-worker from my job in Los Angeles. In fact, it was from Norman, the one I had secretly and briefly dated before leaving the area. He said he was planning to come up to San Francisco and he wanted to see me. *Perfect*, I thought. *This is someone I am fond of and whom I liked.* But even Norman didn't know the truth about my status. He thought I was more experienced. *Should I tell him, I wondered? Would that scare him away?* I decided to play it cool and keep quiet.

Norman arrived and I was excited and yes, a little scared. I was ready for the big night. I purchased a special gown and did all the things I thought one should do for "the first time." I was worried, though, that he'd be able to tell, and I would have to explain. I tried not to think about it. The special night came and, of course, Norman did notice and was upset. He asked me why I hadn't told him. I stalled since I didn't have an appropriate answer. The truth was that I was more focused and disappointed on the lack of fireworks, which made me believe that the first-time stuff had been grossly exaggerated. It would be a while longer before I discovered true fireworks and how a good lover makes all the difference in the world. I never saw or heard from Norman again.

The more I got to know my new boss, the less I liked him. He made rude and nasty comments which flustered me. I was not yet equipped to handle this type of work environment. He was constantly alluding to my physical attributes and asking personal questions. He tried to force me into a sexual relationship which I did not know how to handle at that point. I did not tell Jim about my difficulties with my new supervisor. Instead, on the sly I started searching for another job. I had to get away from Don.

Chapter 5
Meeting an Irishman

I soon found a new position in the Financial District on Montgomery Street for another insurance company with the most startling Irish boss with red hair, fair skin, and striking blue eyes. Born in Boston, Paul was Irish through and through with an incredible sense of humor and love of life. I had never met a true Irishman and no one like Paul, who had five children, three of them hemophiliacs.

He had only one problem, although he didn't consider it an issue. He absolutely loved drinking and the socialization that came along with it. At first, I thought the drinking was related to the serious health conditions of his children. His wife was a nurse and they kept plasma in their refrigerator for emergency situations, so it made sense to me that his children's health was the root cause of the drinking. In the end, I wasn't sure if his family was the reason for his ongoing drinking.

Working for Paul was an adventure. He came into the office only three days a week. Those were drinking days. On those days, we would arrive in front of the *Buena Vista* restaurant at 10:00 am when the doors opened for Irish coffees. And yes, I had to admit they were delicious. After one or two coffees, we would mosey back to the Financial District to visit one of Paul's favorite bars where he had a running tab. Actually, he had tabs in most of the places he frequented. After a drink or two, we might have lunch there or we would go to another location. All the while people would be greeting him wherever we went, saying "Hi Paul!" Everyone knew him.

Shortly after I started working for him, I shyly asked him what the company thought of all these restaurant tabs. "Oh, it's networking," he told me, smiling. "Don't worry." But I did worry. The drinking would continue all day and sometimes included dinner. Paul was a skilled drinker, and he would become gregarious as the day wore on. He often stayed in the city on the days he worked.

Paul loved to sing. Sometimes he wanted to go to Oakland to *The Fat Lady Sings* where they had an open mic in the bar area. I would find a quiet seat in the corner and Paul would sing and wander around talking to other patrons, often buying them drinks. Once in a while, someone would walk over and ask me who I was. When I explained I worked for Paul they would wink and say, "Sure, honey." It was embarrassing, but I got used to it because being with Paul was exciting.

One day after several bar rounds, Paul looked at me and asked, "How about we get some steamers? I feel like steamers today." I had no idea what steamers were, though I feared admitting my ignorance on something he seemed to love. So, I nodded yes and hoped I'd like whatever it was. It was my first experience with clams, and now whenever I eat them Paul and the first time I savored them comes to mind.

Paul loved Dixie music, too. One time he talked me into going to a famous San Francisco establishment known as *The Red Garter*. I had never heard Dixie music live and I wasn't even sure I'd like it.

Paul's car was in the shop, so he asked me to drive. We were unable to find parking anywhere in the area, which is normally the case. Finally, Paul told me to pull into the alley behind the club. "We can park there," he said confidently.

"But, Paul, the signs say it's a towaway zone," I protested. "Oh, don't pay attention to those signs," he said. "They don't enforce them." Worried about my car, I didn't know how to say "no" to Paul, so I hoped he knew what he was talking about.

The place was loud and rowdy with everyone shouting and having a wonderful time. I quickly forgot about my car and started enjoying the music. We were there for an hour and a half and when we exited there was no sign of my yellow Pinto. It had been towed. Sheepishly, Paul said, "They never do that." Too angry, I did not comment but knew from then on I had to be more careful with Paul's assurances.

THE SACRED VOW

On the three days Paul worked, he stayed in the City rather than driving home to Danville. It was because he wasn't in good enough shape to drive. I was often in contact with his wife about his whereabouts. She asked me to let her know if Paul got into trouble. I learned quickly how to monitor my own drinking so that I was in control. It was the only way I could stay sane and safe.

After one all-day drinking session, Paul did not seem like his normal self. He was in bad shape. He had planned on driving home that night, so I talked him into going over to my apartment for some coffee. I feared he could not drive to Danville. He kept saying it wasn't necessary, but I insisted. On arriving, I rushed into the small studio apartment leaving Paul in my studio living room. Once in the kitchen, I hurriedly put on the coffee, wanting to get Paul sober and gone as quickly as possible. I poured the piping hot coffee into a cup and returned to the living room. That's when I saw that Paul had quietly and quickly undressed, folded his clothes neatly on a chair and then had climbed into my small twin bed and fallen asleep. I edged closer to the bed and then tried shaking Paul to wake him up. I shook him several times, but he didn't respond. He was completely out.

Upset and worried, I knew I couldn't stay in the apartment. I was afraid of the subsequent embarrassment surrounding the situation if I stayed. I called my girlfriend, Naida, who lived on the third floor and begged her to let me spend the night in her apartment. "Why can't you stay in your own apartment?" she asked. I explained that my boss was asleep in my bed.

"What? Why is he in your bed?" Naida wanted to know. "Never mind, Naida, I'll explain when I get there," I said hanging up. Grabbing some night clothes, I quietly closed the door behind me.

The next morning Naida and I decided to ring my phone to waken Paul so he would leave. We kept ringing it for a while and then I crept down the stairs to my apartment and let myself in. Paul was gone and the bed was neatly made. He never spoke of the incident, nor did I.

On the days Paul didn't come in, I sat at my desk staring at the phone and willing it to ring. It didn't ring often, probably because most of Paul's business associates knew he was out of the office. No one ever actually came to the office. I'd bring books to read and since there was a bathroom with a shower I'd wash my hair and put it in rollers. All my new women acquaintances were jealous. They couldn't read or set their hair at work.

Everyone knew and loved Paul. In the beginning, not having any work to do was fun; and then I started feeling guilty, especially because on the days Paul was in, we didn't do any work either. When I complained to Paul that I needed to work he would say, "If you're too bored, you could lock up the office and run out and do some shopping. Just don't be gone for too many hours." Not exactly what I was hoping to hear.

I finally came to understand that even though I was being well paid, I couldn't do it anymore. I needed a regular job with real work and less drinking. Paul was upset when I told him. I would always love Paul's enthusiasm and joy for living. He taught me so much about food, being Irish and enjoying life. I tried to stay connected with him, but lost contact when, not surprisingly, he was terminated.

Chapter 6
New Job Worries

My new job was at a large insurance conglomerate not too far from the old location. This time I had three bosses: Doyle, the heavy drinker; Len, the normal guy; and Jim, the lecher. Of course, I didn't know any of this when I took the job. It was a large office space with rows and rows of desks. My three bosses sat directly in front of me. The lecher would ask to sit next to me when he dictated his letters, whispering indiscretions in between the actual letters. He spoke low so the other two could not hear him. Doyle was seldom in the office at the same time as his two associates.

Jim was married and lived in Marin. When he discovered I lived in the Marina, which he passed each night on his way to the Golden Gate Bridge, he made it his business to stop at my apartment and ring my bell. I ignored it. I knew who it was. I asked him to stop, but he did not.

One day, my brother Mike was visiting, and the doorbell started ringing. I ignored it. Finally, exasperated, Mike said, "Hey, aren't you going to get that or least check who it is?" I told him it was my repulsive boss. Jumping up, Mike headed down the stairs and flung open the front door, saying, "Hey, are you looking for someone?" Stunned to see a six-foot male answer the bell, Jim backed away saying, "I must have gotten the wrong number." After that, the nightly doorbell ringing stopped but he continued his lascivious dialogue at work.

Doyle, the sweet but heavy drinker, got into the office by 7:00 am or sometimes earlier so that he could leave by 11:00 am and spend the rest of the day at his favorite hangout, *The Exchange Club*. Everyone else started work at 8:30 am.

Reaching Doyle was always difficult. If I had a question I had to go to *The Exchange Club* or call him there. Getting signatures was problematic as well. Often I would go to *The Exchange Club* and if I had forgotten one of the signature pages, I'd have to go back to the office only to have to return there again to complete the transaction. The bar patrons always looked on in amusement as I tried to balance paperwork while Doyle signed the documents. His wife, too, would call me saying, "I have to reach my husband. He didn't come home last night, and the water pipes broke. Please contact him and tell him to call home."

More distressing was when one of the vice-presidents would come by looking for Doyle and I had to cover for him. I would say he was visiting a customer. "Call him," the VP would demand. "I want to talk to him." Holding the phone as close to my face as possible, I'd dial *The Exchange Club* while the VP stood by. When I asked for Doyle, the bartender would scream out, "Phone call for Doyle Long!" The bar was very noisy and busy, and I was afraid the waiting VP might hear the background noise. Sometimes, Doyle was there and other times he wasn't. In any event, I would cautiously say, "I think he's left. Perhaps he's on his way back." However, Doyle never came back to the office. The VP would stomp off and I would worry for Doyle.

There were drinking parties often on Fridays. They were unpleasant, and the women employees were often treated disrespectfully at these gatherings. The expectation was that the women were there for the benefit of the male employees, so language and sex were treated casually and carelessly. Finally, I decided I couldn't deal with the lecher and *The Exchange Club*, although I was fond of Doyle, who was always a gentleman in a den of wolves.

My friends at the office and I weren't completely innocent. Bored with the ongoing company nonsense, Linda and I were often looking for new adventures. So, when a male employee we liked mentioned he was a Playboy Club member, we pestered him to take us there for lunch. We wanted to observe a real-life bunny in person and see if the place was as decadent as we had been told.

On the appointed day, we left for lunch at our regularly scheduled time, and once inside the club decided to have a drink or two. Soon we were having a fun time and didn't want to return to work; so, we concocted a story that I had become ill, and Linda had to take me home. The net result was that neither of us returned to the office. The next day many employees went out of their way to ask me how I was feeling. They studied me closely. Linda and I assumed word had gotten out about our escapade—from our male cohort. After that, we were treated with a little more deference.

After a year and a half, I decided it was getting more difficult to deal with the lecher and *The Exchange Club*; so late one night after everyone was gone, I slipped a letter of resignation on the vice-president's desk. It was cowardly, but I didn't want to face him and have to answer tough questions—like why I was leaving.

I filed for unemployment, which was denied because the company said I had resigned. I called up the vice-president who had received my resignation letter and told him if he didn't approve it, I would file a formal complaint. I then mentioned some of the things I would include in my complaint, none of which were outlined in my letter. The company approved my claim.

THE SACRED VOW

Chapter 7
More Bad Bosses

Excited and glad to be away from my last employer, I was happy to have found a job in an engineering firm, Tuttle & Bailey. It was in the Ghirardelli Square area and though I hadn't yet gotten to know my new boss, Chuck, I liked the other employees. My earlier experiences made me wary until I had sufficient time to assess my new supervisor.

Chuck was old school and liked to wield his power with the employees, particularly the male ones. They laughed off his quirks. After a couple of months when Chuck felt more comfortable around me, he started telling me jokes, most of them dirty. It made me sick. I didn't laugh but I also didn't say anything. I was a new employee. What could I say if I wanted to keep my job? I also noticed Chuck would take innocent inanimate objects and make them sexual. It shocked and amazed me how he could sexualize a simple telephone.

All of this offended me, so I decided to pay closer attention to the content of his jokes. I had to get him to stop telling me dirty jokes. I didn't care if the others wanted to hear them. I didn't want to hear them. I bought the *Rationale of the Dirty Joke; An Analysis of Sexual Humor* by G. Legman, an eight-hundred-page book on the subject, with an extensive table of contents by subject matter. I read it focusing on his joke predilections.

Finally, I felt ready to confront him. From what I could surmise from the book, his joke interests indicated difficulty with erections. That was a sensitive area, and I knew it was going to be uncomfortable; but I had to do it no matter the consequences. So, the next time he started a joke, I stopped him.

"Chuck," I said, "I'm reading a book called *Rationale of the Dirty Joke* and I'm wondering if what it says is true. Pausing for a moment, I said, "Are you having trouble, you know… with getting it up? Is that why these jokes are so important to you?" Chuck's face turned beet red, and he silently pointed his finger to his exit door. I got the message and left. I had been careful to have this conversation in his office so it would not be overheard, but still I was worried. Had I gone too far or hit too close to home? Chuck never told me another joke—dirty or otherwise. He continued on with the others but left me out of the mix. I didn't get fired and I still have the book.

CHAPTER 8
MEETING ALBERT

Albert and I first crossed paths at Tuttle & Bailey. He came into the office often to see his best friend, Ed; or if Ed was not in, his best friend's girlfriend, Ann. I observed these relationships from afar. Ann was an audacious, friendly co-worker who enjoyed retelling events happening in Ed's and Albert's social group, some of which astonished and embarrassed me. I had a prudish streak, though I tried to hide it. I definitely did not approve of what I heard was going on within the group.

Albert, a ruggedly handsome Italian with a full head of hair, had an energetic personality. He was a friendly guy who always went out of his way to say hello to me, often engaging me in conversation, though I remained aloof. I was definitely not interested in being part of his and Ed's group. After a couple of years of such exchanges we were on friendlier terms. By then I had observed his empathetic listening skills and his generous spirit. However, I still remained reserved and wary around him.

From time-to-time Albert would take me to lunch. Rarely eating much, I'd spend much of the time lamenting over my troubles with my current boyfriend. Albert listened attentively, wisely refraining from providing me with too much advice. Our relationship continued along in this manner for seven years, by which time we had become good friends.

Through the years, Albert had met members of my family. At one point he decided to call my sister for advice concerning upping our relationship from merely friends to something more.

My sister artfully asked, "What does Yolanda say?"

"She tells me it wouldn't work."

"Better listen to her," she counseled.

The lunches continued and during that lengthy period Albert was involved with many relationships, some of which he discussed with me. I didn't ask too many questions as I remained focused on my own relationships.

Albert often held dinner parties for friends. On one occasion he decided he was going to have a party for all his women friends while he was living with his then girlfriend, Peggy. I was invited along with six other women. When I rang the bell with wine in hand, Peggy, a stunning redhead with long, flowing hair and a sprinkle of freckles on her nose, answered. She looked me up and down and in a sharp tone asked, "Which one are you?" Confused, I said, "I'm not sure what you mean. Do you mean girlfriends? If so, I am not one of them. I am just a friend." Peggy studied me for a moment and then widened the door to let me squeeze by her. Her expression told me she didn't believe me.

The party was in full swing, and I saw that Albert's girlfriends were funny, exuberant, some beautiful; and all seemed to love and adore Albert. It was an interesting evening and I thought Peggy might have good reason to be concerned. Dinner was delicious because Albert was renowned for his cooking. As I was leaving I thought about how much I had enjoyed the party and how thankful I was that I wasn't one of "the girlfriends."

Chapter 9
Hospital Woes

Suddenly, in my late twenties, while still working at Tuttle and Bailey, I became quite ill. Worried as my symptoms continued for weeks, I made an appointment with my doctor, a professor at the UCSF Hospital in San Francisco. My only symptom was nightly high fevers which ranged between 102 and 104 degrees. A few minutes into my visit, the doctor insisted I check into the hospital. Flabbergasted and upset, I refused, explaining I had to return to work. "After all," I whined to my doctor, "it is only a fever, nothing requiring hospitalization. I thought I should have it checked out since it has continued for a while." All my arguing was to no avail. My doctor checked me in by phone as I sat nearby fuming. Now, I would have to call my boss, Chuck, and tell him I wouldn't be returning to work. I knew it would infuriate him.

I remained in the hospital for three weeks. During that time, many tests were performed in an attempt to determine the cause of my fevers. In a brief time, the entire length of both my arms were black and blue from the frequent blood draws. The doctors kept insisting on more egregious tests as the negative results piled up. When I first entered the hospital, I was assigned a team of doctors who placed me in the Isolation Ward, fearing I might be contagious.

For heaven sakes, I thought to myself at the time. *I only have a fever.* But I didn't have the courage then to voice these thoughts aloud to my doctors.

Nonetheless, I remained there for a week before I was deemed to be noncontagious and was transferred to the Undiagnosed Ward. The unit's name was later changed because of its negative connotations.

I quickly figured out that many of the patients being brought in from other hospitals with no diagnosis were being placed in my unit. Some died quickly. Others lingered as increased tests were run. It was frightening to watch, and it was getting clearer and clearer to me that the doctors had no idea what was wrong with most of the patients in my ward—and that included me.

One day my physician brought in paperwork for me to sign that would grant them permission to perform a dye test. Afraid, I told them I didn't want to do the procedure. They insisted it might reveal the cause of my fevers, so I reluctantly signed the waiver. Unfortunately, I had a bad allergic reaction to the dye and came remarkably close to needing a blood transfusion to counter the ill effects of the test. And, once again, the results were negative. It seemed to me that my team of doctors was doing every test they could think of in desperation to find something that would explain my fevers.

Soon they scheduled a new test—a bone marrow test which I refused but was again overruled by my doctor. On the day of the test, I was anesthetized but had to be fully awake for the procedure. Seeing the extra-large needle they planned to use troubled me. More alarming was the fact that I could hear my bone crack as the large needle pierced through my chest bone to reach deep down to the marrow. It was a dreadful experience. The test was negative.

I grew increasingly troubled by what was going on in my ward. My skepticism increased each morning as I would awaken panicked that today might be the day they accidentally killed me with their repeated tests. During my entire hospital stay the only prescribed medication I was given was aspirin.

Due to my uncertain and undiagnosed status, I was allowed a lot of freedom, including the right to wander the hospital hallways, which I did every day to relieve my boredom. The only rule I had to follow was that I could not leave the hospital grounds. When I checked into the hospital, I refused to wear the hospital gowns, fearing they revealed too much derriere. Being a modest girl, I was not willing to flash my posterior to strangers. I asked a friend to bring me a nightgown from home. My girlfriend brought only one—a black negligee. *This would have to do,* I thought as I put it on. It was a lovely gown, even if it was long and sexy and hospital inappropriate. If I got cold, I'd toss the hospital gown on top, but the bodice's black lace still peeked out and the gown's long lace edges brushed the floor as I strolled along the corridors.

With no food restrictions and since I did not care for the hospital food, I ordered in as often as I could. One day into my second week, Chuck, who had made no secret that he was suspicious of my claim of being sick after not returning to work, paid me a visit. He sputtered when he saw me in bed saying, "They let you wear that in the hospital?"

"Yes, I'm allowed to wear and eat what I like. Did you bring the hamburger you promised me?" He handed over the burger and fries.

"When are you getting out of here? I can't believe they let you order food in. They really allow that?"

"They don't know what's wrong with me, so I have no restrictions. I'm thinking of leaving next week if they don't discover something. This place is scary. I have to leave. People are dying in my ward. They just disappear and no one says a word. My doctor refuses to let me go. He still thinks he's going to find out what is wrong with me."

I could see he was taken aback by my answer, and I noticed he was trying to restrain from staring at my bodice. Looking away from my chest, Chuck asked, "Well, does that mean you'll be back to work next week? We need you back."

"No, but soon."

He left soon thereafter, I'm sure reflecting to himself how hard it was to believe his employee was really in the hospital and was allowed to enjoy such privileges. He had never heard of such a thing!

Chapter 10
The Goodbye Party

My whole team of doctors visited me often. Many were doctors in training. One of my assigned interns would sit by my bed with a large medical textbook, rifling through the pages searching for a cause of my fever. He had the audacity to do this in front of me, which meant he was actually admitting they didn't have a clue what was wrong.

I had already figured it out anyway. I thought his page flipping was unnecessary and distressing. Growing tired of his daily routine, I asked him outright if my mind could have triggered the fever or if other unsettling things going on in my life could be the cause. Shaking his head, he said, "Absolutely, not. You have a medical condition, not a mental condition." I heard his response but was sure he was wrong. He did not expect a retort, so I didn't reply. By my second week in the hospital, I began to think seriously of leaving and solving the problem myself.

I had an idea of what was causing the fever and it wasn't a disease or a germ. It was a man. Edmund (or Ed, as he liked to be called) became one of my first loves. Our relationship was going nowhere for a variety of reasons. Ed liked me but thought I was too young for him. He would tell me, "I'm thirty years older than you." Yes, I was twenty-six and Ed was a handsome, youngish looking fifty-six because of his ever-present tan and his French and Italian background. Nonetheless, he would get irritated at comments regularly made by others about his age, particularly when he was with me. When we ate out, waiters would often innocently and sometimes not so innocently remark, "I can seat you and your daughter now."

To counter his concerns and outside comments, I cut my hair short and highlighted it white to make me appear older. But, as far as I could discern, he didn't act older than me. In some ways I was the elder. We had met through an advertisement he had placed looking for an *au pair* for his son. He was out of the house a lot working on real estate deals, and I suspect visiting various girlfriends. He wanted someone in the home to watch his son when he was away, so he wouldn't have to worry. Initially, he lived a couple of blocks from the Cliff House, and the proximity to the beach was an additional selling point for me. He later moved to Alameda, where he lived across the street from the beach.

His married daughter did not live at home. On meeting me for the first time, she raised her eyebrows in surprise, because we were actually the same age. She discreetly said nothing other than "Hi," though she had her doubts about me.

At the time I was having financial woes and felt this would be a smart way to save money and catch up. The job came with room and board and a small salary. I was excited about the prospect of saving money and having an opportunity to get more financially stable. I did not expect more.

When we became intimate, I was ecstatic, believing this could be something more lasting. But Ed was always lukewarm towards me. He liked me well enough but continued to see other women whom I considered "floozy types." His first wife (the children's mother) had a drinking problem and had succumbed to her condition ending in her early tragic death. His second wife, whom he had divorced, was still around but was mentally unstable. She was frequently threatening suicide and calling up at all hours requesting money or other help from him.

In my naivete I saw the relationship for more than it was. This reality became evident when I was hospitalized, and Ed refused to come to the hospital to visit. His excuse was that he did not like hospitals. He did call me just once to ask how I was doing. I decided the only way to heal myself was to leave the hospital—and him. Deep in my core, I knew that this was the answer, no matter what the medical experts surrounding me continued to espouse.

THE SACRED VOW

I started planning to leave. Luckily for me, I had my Macy's card, which I always carried in my wallet. I informed my page-flipping intern and all the nurses who would listen that I was having a going-away party on the last Friday of the third week at 5:00 pm. They were all invited. I called Macy's and ordered champagne and champagne glasses. I wasn't sure if anyone would show up. I left a message for my doctor, too. His receptionist called me back and said the doctor would not release me. This response did not deter me in the least. Afraid something bad would happen if I remained in the hospital, I was determined to leave. Scared of the constant tests and the dying people in my ward, I knew I could not stay any longer. I had to get out and away from the hospital!

I called my boyfriend to let him know I was coming home. I did not mention it was only a temporary stay—that I was leaving him. I wasn't even sure he'd care.

When Friday arrived, I was worried the hospital would physically try to restrain me from leaving. Macy's delivered the party goodies on time. I was ready and packed. Soon the magic hour arrived and the first to show up was my intern, who warned me I couldn't leave. "It's dangerous to your health," he cautioned. Smiling, I handed him a glass of champagne, which he took self-consciously. Nurses gathered around me, surprised at my daring but pleased for an opportunity to drink champagne on a workday. To me, it was a celebration. My doctor didn't show, but I hadn't expected to see him.

Looking around at my hospital room one last time, I left at 6:00 pm, ignoring the empty plastic champagne glasses and bottles scattered around the room. It had been a fun though strange going-away party. I jumped into the waiting cab outside the hospital, sighing a deep breath of relief—I was free! I would be well soon.

Once home, my phone began ringing. It was the hospital telling me I did not have authorization to leave and that I had to report back immediately. After answering the first few times, I ignored the ringing for the rest of the evening and in the following weeks. Even my intern called, begging me to come back. I would never return. Surely, they'd gotten that message.

A couple of weeks later I received a letter from my insurance company informing me they would not pay the $5,000 bill because the hospital had failed to make a diagnosis. Quoting the rules, they said that an actual diagnosis was required for payment to be made. This truly angered me. It was not my fault the hospital couldn't figure out what was wrong. I wasn't going back to give them a chance to kill me with their tests. Sighing, I knew I had a big fight ahead of me, but now that I was out the hospital I was filled with renewed energy and ready to take on the fight with the insurance company and the hospital, if needed. I would make them pay if it took every last bit of my strength. After some haggling I got the insurance company to pay.

On returning home, I made plans to move. Within a couple of weeks, I had packed my stuff and relocated to my own apartment. The hospital continued their threatening calls. Once I was home, the fevers stopped completely. It had been a hard lesson —one I would never forget. My idea of medicine and hospitals had been forever changed. I would remain vigilant for the rest of my life concerning all such services, and whenever possible, avoid them entirely. More importantly, I had learned what a powerful tool the mind is and how it could create illness. From that point on and for the remainder of my life, I have always been mindful to monitor my thoughts wisely, especially when it comes to my health. The fevers never returned.

Chapter 11
A New Love

I returned to work and my life minus Ed. Albert was privy to my breakup and had actually visited me in the hospital. Our lunches continued and sometimes we went to dinner. I had moved on to a new love, Peter. Albert listened patiently as I chattered on and on about Peter. I was happy with my new relationship and enjoyed having Albert as a caring friend with whom I could discuss my love life troubles. More at ease with Albert after being friends for more than five years, I shared more of my innermost thoughts outside of my romantic relationships.

My first encounter with Peter was completely accidental.

One evening in mid-January, I met my friend Linda at a local pub in Ghirardelli Square to celebrate my birthday. I was excited to see her. We arranged to meet at 6:00 pm at the restaurant. Linda arrived early. Seeing me enter the restaurant, she waved her arm in the air to draw my attention to where she sat at the bar. I pulled out a stool and sat down. Linda immediately thrust a large 12" x 18" photography book on American Indians by Edward S. Curtis into my arms. It was my birthday gift and is still one of my favorite books. Thrilled with my gift I tried looking through the pictures, but the dim bar light prevented me from seeing them clearly. I put the book aside to order a celebratory drink. The book's considerable size barred me from placing it on the seat next to me. So, I placed it on the counter in front of the empty stool.

Linda and I were having a wonderful time drinking and eating when a man sat down next to me. I heard him but had had my back to him and didn't really pay any attention, at least not until he brusquely asked me to remove the book from the counter. Surprised, I turned around to see a handsome blond man staring at me. Annoyed, I resented his rudely made request. I picked up the book, carefully looking around, unsure as to where to place it next. Finally, I put it on the floor standing up against the bar stool's base. I turned back to my friend, ignoring my new stool mate.

A short while later, the bartender brought over a new round of drinks as we chatted. "Hey, we didn't order a new round," Linda said as he placed the margaritas in front of us. The bartender nodded his chin toward the man next to me and said, "They're on him." I didn't know what to say since I wanted nothing to do with this ill-mannered man. Linda laughed, took one sip, and stood up. "I've got to go," she said, "or I'll miss my train." And with those last words she was gone. I stared at the two full drinks, not daring to look at the stranger sitting next to me.

"Look," he said, trying to get my attention, "I'm sorry if I was rude. I understand it's your birthday. Happy Birthday. My name is Peter. Peter McElroy." I finally turned to look at him. He was smiling, but I could tell he was unsure how responsive I would be. Hesitating and then turning away from him, I picked up my drink and took a long swallow. I wasn't sure I wanted to talk to him, and I didn't normally talk to strangers at bars. "Listen," he said, "you can put your book back on the bar counter if you want. I get you don't want it to get dirty, especially on that floor." Wiping the counter with a bar napkin, he then bent down, grabbed the book, and placed it on the counter in front of him.

I wasn't sure what to say, so I took another long mouthful of my drink. *I am going to drink all these margaritas, I thought to myself. It's my birthday.* The stranger kept trying to engage me in a conversation. Finally, he said, "At least tell me your name. Do you work around here?" I glanced at my gift and thought, "*Oh, what the hell. You can tell him your name and that you work around here. Just don't tell him your last name or where you work.* After an awkward pause, I said, "Yolanda." Picking up my last drink, I hesitated thinking, *I'm not feeling that well*, but I went ahead and took another big sip against my better judgment. Suddenly,

I knew I had to leave. Reaching for my book, I said, "I have to go. I'm sick."

"Frankly, I don't think you should drive," he said. I wanted to argue but felt too ill to debate it, so I walked to the exit with him following closely behind me. I barely made it out the door when I bent over and started vomiting into the bushes right outside the bar. My long hair was dangling in front of my crouched figure when he grabbed my hair and pulled it back in an attempt to hold it away from the watery gush spilling out of my mouth. Thankful and mortified, I stood myself upright. Peter gently held both my elbows saying, "Let me walk you to your car. You should not drive. I can drive you home." *Oh, no, that's not going to happen,* I thought to myself. *I better get myself together if I want to get home to Alameda.*

When we reached my car, he recommended I wait a while before driving home. He even offered to wait with me. I felt better but embarrassed. I just wanted to leave and get away from him. Opening the door to my yellow Pinto, I sat there for a moment taking deep breaths. Standing close to the door, he said, "Please, tell me your full name or at least where you work so I can reach you to see that you are all right."

Shaking my head, I said, "I appreciate your looking out for me, but I have to go. I am sorry about the mess I made," Mumbling ,I continued, "This never happens." Peter reached over me and placed my book he had been carrying on the passenger seat. I closed the door, locked it, and started the car. Suddenly, I turned it off, opened the door, bent over the car ledge, and began vomiting again. Peter stepped back but stood by, quietly watching. "Where do you live? I mean what city? You don't have to tell me your address or anything like that." "I live in Alameda," I muttered.

"You can't drive home over the bridge in your condition. Come home with me and I'll bring you back to the car in the morning. I live in the Mission District, and I promise you nothing will happen to you. You will be safe in my house for the night." I looked at Peter and every alarm went off in my head. *You don't know this man,* I thought. *It's not safe. Do not go with him.* I tried to get out of the car and shake myself to clear my head. I stumbled and Peter grabbed my elbows to prevent me from falling. "Okay," I said, hardly believing I was agreeing to leave with a total stranger. "Please lock your car," he reminded me. "I'll bring you back in the morning."

I tried hard to pay attention to the street names on the drive to his house, but it was dark, and the signs were blurry without my glasses. The name Church Street flashed in front of me when we came to a stop. I remember climbing the steps onto the second story flat and seeing that the walls were papered with some type of large flower. The place smelled musty and had old-fashioned furniture. I wanted to look around to get my bearings but was feeling so wobbly I could only cast a broad glimpse around the flat. Peter saw me glance around and explained, "This is my mom's house. She lets me live here. I live here alone. Let me show you the bathroom. You might want to wash up. I'll put some towels in there for you. You can take a shower if you'd like." I just wanted to sleep. I washed my face. When I returned from the bathroom Peter handed me a glass of water and some aspirins which I gulped down.

I turned towards the bedroom worried but too tired to care. Peter saw my concerned look and said, "Don't worry. I will not do anything. You should get to bed. I sat down on the edge of the bed fretting and wondering where he would sleep. "I only have one bed," he said as he headed for the bathroom. I pulled down the sheet, crawled in and fell sound asleep immediately.

The next thing I knew the sun was shining through the window and I was in bed alone. I knew my body well and it was clear nothing had happened. *Thank you God,* I thought since I had made such an absolutely unsafe choice. Hearing noises downstairs, I scuttled out of bed, rushing to the bathroom to wash my face and rinse out my mouth. The mirror reflected a pale bloated face. Back in the bedroom I noticed my slept in clothing was wrinkled. I felt stinky. I must have taken off my bra before getting into bed because I was not wearing it. Looking around the room I couldn't locate it. I even looked under the bed, but it wasn't there. It was time for me to leave, even if it meant going without my bra. Putting on my shoes, I tiptoed down the carpeted stairs trying not to make a sound. Peter turned and saw me." How are you feeling? Do you need more aspirin? Here, have a cup of coffee. Do you take cream, sugar?" Overwhelmed by the whole situation, I accepted the steaming cup gratefully with a shy smile. I really had to thank him and get out of his home. He had kept his word, though, and for that I was grateful.

"I don't want to rush you," I stammered, "but I really need to get going. I have to get home, change and get to work." Peter studied my ashen face for a moment and said softly, "I'd take the rest of the day off if I were you. You're going to need it." I gulped down the remaining coffee, anxious to leave. Smiling, Peter, said, "Okay, I get the message. I was going to make you breakfast but I see you want to go."

I remained silent as I climbed into Peter's car. I knew I had to thank him, but it was hard getting the right words out. I noticed that he kept his car spotless, reminding me that he had seen my incredibly messy car when he placed my book on the passenger side. I tried out several thank yous in my head, but it hurt so much, and it was hard to concentrate. Finally, without looking at him, I blurted, "Thank you, Peter, for looking out for me and for not taking advantage of the situation. I am so grateful and embarrassed." He nodded slightly, acknowledging my apology.

I couldn't wait to get out of the car and away from him. *Thank God I'll never see him again,* I thought as he dropped me off at my car. I waved a quick goodbye, trying to force a smile. I took two more aspirins when I got home, called in sick and went to bed trying to forget all that had happened on my birthday.

A month later, as I was leaving work, I noticed a piece of paper dangling from my windshield wiper. Grabbing it to throw it away, I saw it was a business card and it had my name on it. It said, "Yolanda, please call me and let me know you are all right. It took me a month to find your car to leave this card. I just want to see that you are okay." It was signed 'Peter.' Shocked, I tore up the card into little pieces and put it in my pocket. *That's never going to happen,* I thought. *It would be too embarrassing. What could I say? Nope, not happening,* I whispered to myself.

A week later there was another business card on my windshield. "Please call me. There is no need to be embarrassed. I would like to see you." I tore up that card, too, and decided to park my car further down the street or on the next street. Then maybe he wouldn't find it.

On Thursday, when I returned from lunch, Chuck intercepted me and handed me a bag saying, "A man left this for you while you were out." His enigmatic smile was puzzling, so I dared not open the bag in front of him. Instead, I headed for my desk and waited for an opportunity when he was no longer watching me. I opened my typewriter case and started typing, pretending not to notice his observation. As soon as I saw he'd lost interest in watching me, I bent down and pulled the bag from under my desk. Who had left it? And why? I had no idea, but I was troubled by Chuck's piqued interest. I opened the bag and quickly closed it, too stunned to figure how he had found me. The bag contained a beautiful live pink rose and my bra. *Oh, what my lascivious boss must have thought,* I wondered. *This was too much.*

The following week there was no card from Peter, and I thought moving my car had done the trick. But I remained worried since he now knew where I worked. On Friday, there was another card and message: "Yolanda, please call me. I want to take you out to dinner. Please don't move your car. I finally figured out where you work. You had told me it was an engineering firm but had refused to give me the name of the company. Lucky for me, there aren't that many engineering firms in the Ghirardelli Square area. "Anyway, I left a package at your work. Did you get it? Peter."

Frustrated, I didn't know what to think. He had seen me at my worst and yet he still wanted to invite me to dinner? That alone was amazing. This time I didn't tear up the business card. Instead, I put it into my pocket. *Surely,* I told myself, *you're not thinking of calling him. I have to think about it. He was handsome and I loved his voice, but it would be awkward to see him. Should I apologize for throwing up all over the bushes and all over his shoes? Making his house stinky? No, better to pass on the dinner,* I mused.

The next week my windshield bore another card: "Don't be shy. I'd like to see you. How can I convince you to have dinner with me? Peter." I didn't know what to think. He wasn't giving up. I studied the business card. I'd call and see what happened. Returning to my desk and making sure no one was within hearing distance; I dialed the first number. I got a switchboard and hung up rather than asking for him by name. I tried the second number. He answered, "Peter McElroy."

Stammering, I wondered if he'd remember who I was, "It's... it's Yolanda." For a quick second I thought he wouldn't respond but then he quickly said, "Are you all right? I know it was a while back, but I worried about your getting home."

"Yes, I'm fine," I told him. "Good, I'd love to take you to dinner." Before I could get a word in to tell him I couldn't go to dinner, he continued, "Do you know Buena Vista? Do you want to meet there? It's near your work, so I am hoping it would be a good place to eat. Can you meet me on Friday at 6:00 pm?" I knew I should have said I couldn't meet him and asked that he stop leaving notes on my car, but I was thrilled with his restaurant choice as it was one of my old hangouts with Paul. Peter, of course, didn't know that.

But there was still the meeting part. Could I face him? Silent for a moment, I said, "Well, I am not sure..." Peter quickly interjected, "It's just dinner. If you don't enjoy my company, I'll stop leaving notes on your car."

The dinner date came, and I was extremely nervous, feeling awkward about seeing someone who had seen me in such a messy and deplorable state. I dressed carefully and arrived a few minutes early to try to calm myself. I kept reminding myself it would be okay. Peter had seen me in a horrible state. Now, he would see me at my best, or at least looking better than the last time we met. The restaurant was unusually crowded, but Peter was able to find me despite the bustling crush of people. He sat down and smiled. Taking a deep breath, I smiled, suddenly feeling my heart tremble. *Perhaps it will be okay,* I thought. Thus began our relationship.

Chapter 12
The Job Offer

Peter kept telling me he could get me an excellent job where he worked making union wages. He offered to speak to his boss about setting up an interview. I declined knowing how our relationship had been going. I thought it would be too difficult working at the same company. Peter explained it would be for the same company but that he worked at a different location. The money was definitely tempting, but I still wasn't sure it was a good idea.

Finally, I agreed to an interview with Peter's boss, Dick. The scheduled interview was at lunch at La Traviata the Mission district, near the work location. This arrangement set off alarm bells in my head, but I said yes because I had promised Peter I would follow through on his referral. Afraid, I knew I might have to give my potential employer my speech about not dating people I worked with. Anyway, it wouldn't come to that. Peter had said Dick was married so perhaps I was worrying for nothing.

The dark, Italian restaurant made me nervous. It was not the normal interview location. Dick was quite friendly. Once seated and with a drink in hand, Dick first questioned me about Peter. He wanted to know what my relationship was with Peter. "We're friends, that's all," I said, remembering Peter's caution about not telling Dick about our relationship. "Good," he said. I wasn't sure why that was the case.

I knew then I was going to have to give him my little speech, so everything was out in the open. I was terrified that it would be embarrassing and would result in losing a job opportunity. This would be the first time I would confront a potential employer head on, and I wasn't sure I had the courage to do it. Taking a deep breath, I pushed on.

"Dick, I really feel I have to tell you something before I start working for you. Looking directly at him, I said, "I make it a point to never go out or see anyone I work with." I knew I was seeing Peter, but I had met him before considering working there. Yes, I recognized it was a fine line.

Dick sat up straighter and said, "What makes you think anyone would be interested in you? It's presumptuous for you to assume I am interested in you." His words were meant to shame me; and they did; but I was sure I had read the cues right. After all this time I had learned a thing or two about bosses. Should I respond to his mean comment? It had been difficult enough giving my speech. Actually, it was the hardest thing I had ever done, and having it thrown back in my face was hard to take. Taking another deep breath, I said, "Well, I feel it is important that you know my policy so there won't ever be any confusion." He was silent for a couple of minutes, and I felt sure he would revoke the job offer. *It was just as well if he's going to be a problem*, I thought. He stared at me for a moment and asked if I was ready to go. What did that mean? I was confused.

Walking out into the blinding sunlight after the dark restaurant was startling. Dick turned to me and said, "See you on Monday at 9:00 am" as he walked off. I didn't know what to think. It was so disconcerting. Now I was having serious second thoughts about the job. He might be another problem boss, but I had promised Peter I would consider it.

Later that evening Peter called to ask how it went. I told him I got the job. I didn't mention my little speech but did tell him that Dick had asked about him and I said we were only friends. Peter was excited. I was troubled about working with Dick and Peter. The only good thing about the new job was the remarkably high salary. *You can do this,* I told myself.

On Monday I showed up early and noticed the other office workers were staring at me and not in a particularly friendly way. My new supervisor came over, introduced herself, and turned to look at the other staff. "Don't pay too much attention to them. They don't like it when someone gets hired as an inside job." *Inside job*, I thought, *I'll have to see how this goes. If I don't like it, I'll quit.*

My relationship with Peter continued to be a secret. He would send me love notes via interoffice mail since he was at a different location. I was concerned that someone would look in the envelope and see the sealed envelope marked *personal* and look inside. Peter wrote the sweetest love letters, especially after we had an argument. I still have all his letters and notes. He knew I loved orchids, so he would leave a cut orchid on my desk; and if we had a fight, I would receive an extraordinarily beautiful one.

Three weeks after starting the job, Peter asked me to go to Hawaii with him on vacation. I wanted to go, but how could I? I had just started the job and it would look strange if we both came back with a tan. I told Peter I didn't see how it was possible. A couple of days later Dick casually mentioned that Peter was going to Hawaii with a girlfriend. I knew Dick shared this information purposely to see how I'd respond.

I smiled but was crushed. As soon as I could I made a beeline for the restroom, where I held my hand over my mouth as I wept in one of the stalls. This was the beginning of a game Dick would play over and over to torture me.

In between telling me about Peter whenever he could, Dick would make inappropriate sexual comments. I wasn't sure I could cope. Peter's and my relationship was on and off, my co-workers barely spoke to me, and my boss was impossible. I had to find a way to deal with Dick. I decided I would react to his inappropriate sexual comments with crazy responses. So, whenever he started in, I would say, "Yes, the sky is pretty blue today, don't you think so? And before he could respond I would go on and on about the weather. Puzzled, he'd stop my diatribe saying, "I don't know what you're talking about." It was clearly frustrating him, so I thought it might work, and from that time on I would go on and on about inane subjects whenever he started his unacceptable comments. It slowed him down but did not stop him entirely.

I learned soon after starting that, like many of my past bosses, Dick was a heavy drinker. Dick would go drinking with his friends and lose his car on a regular basis. He would come into the office the next morning and ask me to call the police department to see if I could track it down. He, of course, had no idea where he had lost it. Surprisingly, he never seemed overly concerned about his car. It was insane spending time finding his lost car repeatedly. He had so many tickets the police department knew his car and license plate by heart. They laughed when I called.

After working for a period of time on the job Dick said we were going out into the field. I didn't know what that meant, but I didn't like the idea. As I grabbed my purse, my supervisor stopped me and asked if I had locked everything up. "No, we're coming back," I replied. "No, you're not," she said. "No one comes back when they go in the field with Dick. Lock the files and the office." *This is ridiculous,* I thought to myself. *Why do I keep getting these alcoholic bosses who only want to spend their time drinking?* My supervisor was right. We did not come back until after 5:30 pm, after the office had closed.

When we arrived back in the parking lot, Dick said, "There is a neat bar right around the corner. Let's go." I stalled, saying I had to get home, but he said, "It'll be a quick one. I think you'll find it interesting." I knew I should go home. These excursions were getting to be too much.

The bar rendered me speechless. I had never seen anything like it. It featured a long counter on the left that ran the entire length of the facility. Stools sat in front of the bar counter. It was very crowded but most of the patrons were not seated. Instead, they stood in front of their stools, two and three deep. This enabled them to thoroughly inspect all the new bar entrants. Some glanced admiringly at Dick. Others made lewd comments as we walked past. I was too busy staring at the wall above the bar to listen closely. The wall featured dozens and dozens of neck braces, hanging whips and chains in all lengths and sizes. I knew it was rude to stare, but it was an incredible display. I was trying to figure out what some of the items were, so I did not listen closely to the men complimenting my boss. *Yes, he was handsome, but he is definitely an asshole,* I murmured to myself.

Intrigued, I finally looked around and noticed there were no women in the bar except me. Then I knew what kind of a bar it was.

THE SACRED VOW

No one looked at me. We sat down at a table in the back. Clearly, Dick knew this place. I just wanted to stare at the chains but thought better of it. I surreptitiously glanced at Dick, who was ignoring all the looks directed his way. There were many men in the bar: young ones, very handsome ones, rough looking ones, older guys, and some movie star lookers. I wanted to laugh out loud, but thought it was best not to. This was the final blow. *I am going to have one drink and get the hell out of here and I have to get out of this job,* I promised myself.

In the meantime, things were not going well with Peter. One day he was a devoted lover and then a couple of days later he would pull away and say we should take a break. It was maddening and I didn't know what was going on with him from day-to-day. I wanted to quit but was afraid to leave the job.

One day Dick called me into his office saying excitedly that he had just got a huge promotion and was moving to Los Angeles. I was secretly ecstatic. His next sentence startled me. "I want you to come with me. It will be a huge promotion for you, too." *I couldn't believe it. Why would I ever want to go anywhere with him and how would he not know it? This is the time to speak your truth* I told myself. Albert had recently asked me to move in so I wouldn't need the job. *Tell him,* my conscience urged. *Tell him now!* Sighing and trying to get up my courage, I said, "I appreciate your asking, Dick, but I would never go with you to Los Angeles. Working for you has been difficult and uncomfortable." Dick actually had the nerve to look surprised by my comments and went on to say, "Well, here's my new address in case you change your mind."

Men, I thought, as I walked out of his office.

Chapter 13
Albert Again

After one luncheon I shared my secret wish with Albert. I had not disclosed it to anyone as I was self-conscious about expressing it out loud. I desperately wanted to go to college. Two concerns were holding me back—specifically, my age (I was afraid I was too old at 32) and my ability to pay for full-time schooling. Things with Peter continued to be up and down. Even though I was desperately in love with Peter, he continued to pull away from me whenever we got emotionally close. He would then return after a brief period of time, devoted as ever. The mantra he kept repeating was, "It isn't you, but other things I am wrestling with." I was suspicious there was another woman but had no proof. The relationship was breaking my heart. Lunches with Albert were spent dissecting the relationship and trying to figure out how to fix it.

Things with Peter ended badly. Albert knew some of the details, but I did not reveal the one that devastated me—that Peter had left me for another man.

During one late night dinner, Albert suggested I move in with him, stop working and go to school full-time as I wanted. He was not living with anyone at that time and his most recent love had moved out. I was not privy to the reason. Overwhelmed and thrilled by the prospect, I wanted to say yes but then remembered my reluctance about furthering our relationship. We had been such good friends through the years. I didn't want to ruin our special connection. I was worried the invitation would take the relationship to a new level, or at least that seemed a possibility.

I knew about the other women, and I wasn't even sure if he was asking me to start a relationship or if he was just being kind and helping a friend go to school. I suspected it was the former since he had tried to elevate our relationship several times before and I had gently resisted, always saying it wouldn't work out. I told him how much I appreciated his offer but had to think about it. Meanwhile, in my heart all I could think about was that this was my chance to fulfill my longtime dream of going to college.

With trepidation and hopes it would work out, I took Albert up on his offer and moved in with him. There was a lot of discussion among Albert's friends that I was using Albert, but he had asked me to move in. I had not tricked him, and it had never really occurred to me that he would make such an offer. He had always been supportive of my continuing my education. Living with him allowed me to follow my dream and did help me out financially. Still, it hurt that some of his friends thought I was taking advantage of him.

It appeared that we were to have an intimate relationship and secretly I was thrilled, but scared. I hoped it would work out.

Chapter 14
School Days

UC Berkeley was not my first choice of colleges. I wanted to attend a smaller, more intimate school environment. I was insecure and not sure how I'd do in school with younger and what I thought were smarter students, so I applied to a number of schools. I was accepted and offered a full scholarship to the University of Pacific (UOP), one of the oldest chartered universities in the western United States. I accepted the offer and made plans to visit the campus and attend an open house. Albert accompanied me. As we wandered among the grove of trees and chatted with other prospective students and UOP professors, I discovered something that made me change my mind.

I no longer remember the professor's name or what he taught but I will always remember his comments. We introduced ourselves using only our first names, and I explained how excited I was to be able to attend UOP. It was apparent the professor did not catch my first name or understand its significance because it is unlikely he would have made his subsequent comments concerning Hispanics. He immediately lamented the entrance of so many Hispanics into the college saying that many of them were not fully qualified. His dislike for that group of students rang through his conversation. Shocked, I looked at Albert, who nodded his head silently in acknowledgement that we should leave. I didn't respond to the professor's racist comments because I couldn't believe that he would make such statements, at least not in an open house setting. It was clear he did not understand I was Hispanic. I backed away, grabbing Albert's hand while telling the professor we had to leave.

Upset, I made my way back to the car, remembering all the things I should have said but didn't. I knew then I would never attend that school and decided to write a letter of protest to the administration. My letter quoted the professor directly, and then I advised the school I was declining the full scholarship I had accepted. UOP responded to my letter offering an apology along with an even better schoolarship. I did not reply.

I knew then I would have to attend UC Berkeley, which some would say was not such a bad option. To me it was a big and scary choice, although it turned out for the best in the end. UC Berkeley taught me so much more than specific knowledge in individual subjects. It taught me how to master and maneuver through systems no matter what type of blockages existed. The value of that skill and the knowledge to manage challenges far out surpassed any content garnered from the many classes I took while there.

My college curriculum also required outside field work. I selected Legal Services because I thought that organization would help me get into law school. At that time, I was considering going to law school and at that point still believed law school was about bringing justice to the forefront. I worked in a volunteer capacity for a year, and then I was hired as an employee while still in school.

My clients were poor, often uneducated, and in need of all types of social services besides the legal advice I was able to provide. I came to love them and the quiet dignity they displayed in the face of so many challenges. Their unwavering dignity showed through even in front of uncaring judges. There was many a time when I had to place their phone calls on hold to prevent myself from bursting into tears as they relayed a lengthy list of heartbreaking troubles, many which were not easily resolvable.

Our individual caseloads were tremendous because many Social Security cases were automatically denied on the first step. I worked in an old downtown Oakland building located on Telegraph and Seventeenth Street. It was an unsafe location, both inside and outside of the building. This environment added to the stress of an already overwhelming job. For safety reasons, the building was kept locked at all times, as were each of the individual offices and the restrooms.

THE SACRED VOW

Employees were warned to never walk alone in the hallways because of the recurring building shootings.

I was required to appear in front of various administrative law judges on behalf of Legal Service clients. My task was to challenge the denial of their Social Security benefits and to request full reinstatement along with repayment of any lost money. In that role I was able to observe the judges up close, learn their interests in certain types of injuries and notice their biases. Several were disdainful of those appearing in front of them and it showed in the disrespectful way they spoke to the denied recipients. Some of the administrative law judges were sympathetic of my clients' plights and two judges would later write reference letters for me for law school.

I had many unusual and disturbing hearings. Two cases in particular weighed heavily on me as I look back. One involved a short, middle-aged, shy Mexican woman with a severe back injury who had been denied benefits. Clients were required to appear at the hearings along with their legal counsel. I had to prepare her for the judge's questions. Her case would be in front of a judge who asked very personal questions on all back injury cases. They were normally of a sexual nature.

Though she spoke limited English I hesitated, not knowing how to explain what she would have to say to win. Afraid of offending her, I knew I had to discuss her sexual relationship with her husband because this judge would ask. I inquired if she knew what the *missionary position* was. She shook her head. I explained it was a sexual position and since I didn't speak fluent Spanish I used my hands to demonstrate the pose. I disclosed that when the judge asked her in what position she had sex with her husband she would have to tell him it was never in the *missionary position*. If he asked further questions, I advised her to tell him she performed oral sex on him and that she never had sex lying on her back because of the severe pain.

Uncomfortable and upset, she said, "I can't discuss such things with a stranger. "Why would he ask such questions?" Worried she wouldn't be able to handle the queries. I had her practice with me. Nervously she looked down at her hands each time she said the words, *"oral sex,"* clearly upset to have to discuss such intimate parts of her life to get the Social Security benefits due her. The judge's first question, as expected, concerned her sexual practices with her husband. She spoke softly but said all the right words, though I could tell she was terribly embarrassed. The judge ruled in our favor rather than have me contest his denial.

The second case concerned a woman who had had a brain tumor that had not healed properly. The indentation on the right side of her head was clearly visible. She did not look well. She had been in front of this judge before. When interviewing her I discovered she was on welfare and had done a little prostituting on the side to get money for food. I suspected she drank but did not ask her about it. I knew this judge had a problem with clients on welfare even though that was not an adequate reason for denial of benefits. I was worried she would not be able to hold her own at the hearing with the assigned judge.

We made plans to meet right before the hearing so we could go over everything again. Dressed better than usual, she held on tightly to an exceptionally large tote bag. She said she had to use the restroom. We didn't have much time, so I followed her in, trying to relay last minute directions. Once we were in the bathroom, she opened the tote and pulled out a large bottle of vodka, unscrewed the cap and took a large swig before I could stop her. "Stop," I screamed. She looked over at me but continued drinking. I tried to reach for the bottle, but she moved away. Upset, I said, "Put it away now. You can't be drunk when we go into the hearing." Wiping her mouth with her sleeve she put the bottle back in her purse.

She followed me out into the courtroom. Worrying this would not go well, I thought that my only chance to win might be to get the judge to say something incriminating about welfare or exhibit some other type of bias. All the hearings were taped so my mere request for copy after the hearing would alert him I planned to challenge his decision.

His first question astounded me and told me he knew her well. "How many drinks have you had so far today?" I held my breath. Using her hand as a measure, she said, "Ah, just a couple." " I'm asking you again," he said more sternly, "How many?" She then took the bottle out of her purse showing him the remaining contents. I was upset with her at this point. "Put the bottle away," he said. "What about your benefits? Are you still on welfare?" *Oh, no. Here we go again.* "Yes, your honor," she said. He shook his head. Then something snapped and he made several snide inappropriate remarks about people on welfare. Saying a silent prayer, I thought *Alleluia*. Now I had a chance to win her benefits back. He then started asking her if she was still working the streets.

Hell, I thought to myself. This hearing is going downhill quickly. I was agitated, trying to restrain myself from pulling her out of the room. "Not anymore," she said. His expression revealed he did not believe her. I just wanted the hearing to end before any more damage could occur.

Smiling, I requested her benefits be reinstated and then said, "And I'd like a copy of today's tape. Thank you." The judge looked at me knowing what that meant. He couldn't deny my request. Rather than allow me to challenge his unfavorable decision, he ruled in our favor.

But it didn't end there. Dennis, my boss at Legal Services, wanted me to file charges against the judge *for abuse of power*. I refused. Dennis insisted. I knew nothing would come of it and that judge had given me a letter of reference for law school. Dennis scheduled a meeting with me. I had my letter of resignation in front of me on the desk, upside down so it could not be read. Dennis sat down across from me giving me all the reasons why I should file the complaint. I had won my case and I liked my biased judge. We both knew these types of complaints never went anywhere. The judge was upfront about his biases, which helped me win cases. I told Dennis I wouldn't do it. He looked at me unhappily. I volunteered to resign so the Agency could file on my behalf. It was then that I turned my letter over and handed it to him. He read it and then tore it up. "Forget it," he said as he walked out. I continued working there.

Meanwhile at school, Berkeley continued to expose me to innovative ideas and people who came from a different environment than mine. The classes were varied and some, as one in Economics and another on Human Sexuality, were shocking.

One afternoon as I sat in my small section Economics class, I listened in astonishment at the comments made by my fellow students. We were discussing the causes and outcomes of poverty. Most students focused on the material side of poverty. I was seething but didn't want to speak up. I looked at the teacher and thought he would expand the discussion to a microeconomic level. But no, he allowed the students to continue debating why some people remained poor despite aid and other services offered to them.

Finally, I reluctantly raised my hand. Upset and angry at this point, I looked around the room. Yes, I knew most of the students were from a more privileged background than myself, one that allowed them to attend a prestigious university such as Berkeley. *But still*, I thought, *surely they must have more awareness of others' situations dissimilar to theirs.*

I could hardly hold back my words as I said, "Poverty is more than not having food or shelter. It is about a loss of hope and spirit. It is about the failure to see the possibility of something better. It wears you down and eats away at your very soul. It causes you to make bad decisions out of desperation. It makes you ashamed. It does not allow you to even understand the concept of deferred gratification. The worst part of it is that the memory follows you throughout your life no matter how successful or how much money you make. You still remember the feelings of lack and shame for years into the future. So, please understand me when I say this is so much more than material loss. I know because I lived it."

There was a hushed silence when I finished. No one looked at me or spoke to me. I regretted speaking up but couldn't help it. The bell rang. and the teacher looked around and without further comment said, "Class is dismissed for today."

Right before graduation the Dean's Office notified me I was short one class credit to complete my undergraduate degree. Upset, I looked over the possible class options and thought the Human Sexuality class sounded interesting. I had to sign up for the class in one of the Administration Building foyers. A handsome young guy came in and stood behind me in line for the sign-up sheet. Motioning him to go in front of me, I said I was still deciding. He then asked, "Do you think being gay is a political statement?" Surprised by the question, I thought *no, it's a choice*. Looking at him, I said, "I don't think so." By the end of the class, I discovered I was wrong.

On the first day of class about three hundred students were enrolled. At the end there were less than thirty. The professor explained he would be the moderator but that the actual class would be run by a panel of student experts. I wasn't sure what that meant. We were given a syllabus which covered the background on the gay movement starting with the Stonewall riots in 1969 and its legacy, though there was a long history before that period. Gay writers were prominent on the list. The teacher explained that different panels would discuss every aspect of the movement from religious leaders to parents to health professionals and activists.

I had thought the class would be broader and include all types of sexuality, but now realized it was solely focused on the gay movement. I figured I'd stick it out even though I could see there were some politicized groups in the class that would be taking strong, strident positions on all the topics discussed.

The first panel was a religious one consisting of a priest, a rabbi, a nondenominational clergy, and an Episcopalian. The discussion included each one's views on same-sex attraction. It was fascinating to hear the different religious denominations' responses to the movement and to the individual panelists. Some were more tolerant than others. All strove to appear impartial though some religions opposed such relationships.

The health panel shared data on human sexuality, explaining how individuals could fall on a continuum that could move from one end of the spectrum to the other in a lifetime. This was often by choice or circumstance. Some people, they explained, were born knowing their preference. Others were uneasy and unsure of their proclivity and because of societal/family environments were not free to show their inclination. There were detailed discussions about those who elected to physically change their gender and the medical and societal pressure associated with such choices.

The parent panel intrigued me the most. It included parents who fully supported their child's choice and others who were adamantly opposed for religious or other reasons. One mother told a heartbreaking story about how she had rejected her son when he told her of his preference for men. Later realizing her error, she spoke of the road back to accepting and loving him unconditionally. She explained how she was now committed to educating other parents in similar situations.

The class size kept dwindling as the strong, assertive groups attempted to control the dialogue and flow of certain topics. Some of the women in the class said they wanted nothing to do with men. They said they would not allow men even to enter their homes. Their contempt for men leaked out as they spoke passionately about not allowing men to play any role in their lives. To me, as a woman who thought she knew where she fell on the sexual spectrum, their antagonism was disconcerting. The fact that the professor or moderator, as he called himself, did nothing to move the class towards more impartiality or at least the appearance of it, left me frustrated. The professor simply let the class blunder along. More students dropped out. I remained in the class but felt alone and out of place. I had to graduate, and couldn't wait for another quarter, so I remained enrolled. And, I had to admit I was learning a lot.

However, when the class was asked to do a paper on a topic of our choice concerning sexual orientations, I felt elated to finally be able to dive into the topic at a deeper, nonpolitical level. My paper would be on American Indian shamans who pretended to be pregnant. Through an established ritualized practice within the tribe, they reenacted the entire nine months of a normal pregnancy. I researched the subject thoroughly and was pleased with my paper. After submitting what I considered an "A" paper, I was furious when I got a "B" plus. I went to the professor requesting he review my paper and change the grade. He refused, saying I had to go to the panel who had done all the grading. I spoke to them, and they declined to change the grade, saying I had used the sexist pronoun "he." But, I protested, "they were male shamans!" Nonetheless, they said because of my use of the word "he" they would not change it. I returned to the professor, who shrugged his shoulders and told me to let it go.

By the end of the class there were few heterosexuals left. Two, I knew of for sure: me and the professor who wouldn't speak up.

Chapter 15
The Psychic's Prediction

In the beginning all had seemed well with Al. I started school, was happy, and Albert continued his routines and duck-hunting activities. Al's former girlfriends were still around as he had always maintained long-term relationships with all his former girlfriends, so it did not seem strange to me. They were invited often to the house for dinners and were involved in many of our activities, including clamming parties and get-togethers to celebrate holidays and friends' birthdays. He seemed happy with our relationship, or at least that was my perception.

During this time one of the amazing things I learned from Albert was to cook with joy. Albert was an exacting foodie. Before I had met him I fancied myself a good cook. However, I soon discovered I really didn't have the expertise or knowledge that he possessed, and I was surely not anywhere as good as I had believed. At our first dinner together, he served wild pigeon with spaghetti. Albert only used fresh spices, no garlic powder. Sauces and dressings were made from scratch, so no bottled salad dressings or pasta sauces could be found in his house. Albert didn't normally use recipes but did on some occasions as a reference point. When I asked him how he made a certain thing he would say, "Use a little of that and a little of that," not too helpful in my mind! I learned the only way I could by observing him as he prepared his different specialties. He even made his own pasta from scratch. This skill was not something I yearned to learn, but I did at one time make dozens and dozens of homemade ravioli and pesto sauce from scratch with him.

The relationship had bumps in the road and many of those clashes involved other women. I normally didn't consider myself the jealous type, but I was becoming increasingly so in my current environment. I lost trust in Albert and was deeply hurt. I had assumed that we had a more committed relationship. But in the following years, it became clear that Albert's interest had waned considerably and that he was maintaining other outside relationships. I wasn't even sure if they were short-term or long-term. When questioned about them, he continued his pattern of denial, which wounded me further. By the time my college graduation rolled around, the relationship was rocky, and both of us were eager to part.

Nonetheless, Albert graciously held a graduation party for me in Tilden Park, inviting friends and my family to help celebrate my accomplishment. It was supposed to be a special day with a picnic in the park and then everyone returning afterwards to our home for cake and ice cream. People streamed into our small El Cerrito home offering their congratulations. Al went to get the cake which had been stored in the downstairs refrigerator. Noticing that Albert hadn't returned, I went downstairs and found Albert and a former girlfriend in a compromising position. They separated quickly on seeing me coming down the stairs. "The cake?" I asked. "Oh," Albert said. "Tule (his dog) had gotten into it and eaten part of it. We've been trying to patch it up." It was clear both parties had been distracted with other business than fixing the cake. I glanced at the girlfriend, who smiled and said they would be right up. She then held up the disheveled cake as further evidence that this was the reason for their delay.

Though upset, I was not surprised. However, it was my special day so it pained me that they couldn't wait and at least be out of my presence. It confirmed what I already knew—a truth I had always known from the beginning and that I had tried so hard to ignore. I wanted out and for all I knew it was highly likely he wanted me gone too.

Frustrated with the difficulties of the relationship and all the women, I scheduled an appointment with a recommended Sufi psychic, eager for answers on how to proceed. Written questions were submitted to the psychic prior to a scheduled phone call. There would be no face-to-face meeting and the taped phone conversation would be sent to me for future reference. I still have the tape. I had specific questions regarding money for law school and how to get Albert out of my life. I felt that living with him was hell and I wanted out.

Anxious to get the answers, I was cranky and unsure if I would get any information that would help me make the critical decisions facing me. Finally, the day arrived. The reading stunned and astonished me, as answers to questions I never asked were provided.

The psychic began by describing a detailed floor exercise she saw me doing daily, explaining it was part of my self-care routine. This knowledge surprised me but not as much as when she went on to say that one person in the relationship had a drinking problem. "It's not you. It's one of the reasons you are together," she said. I was flabbergasted. No one knew about Albert's drinking. He had hidden it so well that I had only recently found out about it by accident. However, this was not one of my queries, so it was remarkable that the psychic had picked it up.

I tried to stifle my impatience, wondering when the psychic would get to my question about moving on and away from Albert. The intuitive revealed another astounding and upsetting fact. She said that I would have a child and it would be a boy. She continued on, saying, "You will be the type of mother who expects the absolute best from your child; so, you'll tend to nag that child to ensure he always does his best. You will have exacting standards and therefore have elevated expectations for him."

"No, I don't think so. That's not in my plan," was my snappish reply.

"You don't know how these things work," the medium said quietly.

"Yes, I do, and it won't happen," was my frustrated retort.

This information troubled me since it was not on point as I had not asked about children. Why would this topic even come up? I just wanted to know how to get Albert out of my life. The seer went on to describe the many lifetimes Albert and I had shared—as brothers in Ireland, as sisters, some as a married couple with children and other lives as lovers. "But," she said, "this lifetime was about your most recent one in France, where you were married. Both of you lied and cheated throughout your marriage. You didn't hate each other. You stayed together but were completely indifferent to each other by the end. This lifetime is about learning to tell each other the truth. You know each other at a very deep level. You will end up being close friends this time, once you tell each other the truth."

I didn't believe that was possible and said, "I don't know about any of that. I just want him out of my life. Please tell me how to do that." The medium continued, "That's not going to happen. He will be in and out and the relationship will fizzle down at times, but he will remain a constant throughout your life."

"Wait!" she said, "I see a little ribbon above your relationship revealing there will be one more shared lifetime at which time you will be good friends, and that will be the ending of your cycle together." Though interesting, none of this information pleased me. The intuitive went on to explain that the financial strings that were concerning me would not stop me from continuing my education at law school if that's what I wanted.

Unfortunately, the critical piece of information the psychic did not reveal was that I would have "the child" with Albert. Did she purposely fail to tell me who the father would be? On the other hand, I didn't ask. At the time I didn't even believe the information, quickly dismissing it since I was not going to have children. In fact, I would never have made the connection that our child was the reason Albert would remain in my life since he couldn't have children, we were not intimate, and I was not planning on children or staying with him.

I later shared some of the psychic's information with Albert, particularly about our former lives in France and Ireland and his drinking. I did not mention the psychic's prediction that I would have a child. Albert did not seem too interested or impressed.

After a lot of soul-searching and hearing that the financial strings would not stop me, I decided to go to law school. I applied and was accepted at several schools. I did not want to return to L.A., so UCLA was out of the question, though I was reluctant to pass up such a good school. I decided to go to Davis, which was closer to the

THE SACRED VOW

Bay Area. I was offered an opportunity to do a law intern program in Tacoma, Washington, a month before school started in August. Excited, I accepted the invitation to attend.

Albert volunteered to drive me there because he was interested in exploring some asparagus farms in the area as an investment. We had officially broken up but the prospect of getting a ride there made sense to me, so I accepted. It was a long trip as we crisscrossed the states of Oregon and Washington. It was the last time we were intimate, something that had not occurred in a long while. Albert dropped me off and returned to the Bay Area. On my return, I would report to Davis to start law school.

Despite the challenging times, Albert had always been generous with me, and he had openheartedly given me the opportunity to fulfill my childhood dream of going to college. He had many redeeming qualities but was not a good partner for me. But hadn't I known this from the beginning? I could not deny it had been obvious from the earliest days. Was I like so many other women who hoped to change their man or who secretly trusted it would work out somehow? Clearly I fell into the latter category since I was fully aware of Albert's numerous romantic liaisons. How could one woman be so wrong?

Chapter 16
To Be or Not to Be

Law school started and my relationship with Albert was officially over. He was refocusing on his steady girlfriend, who was moving in with him. By early September I was not feeling well, which was unusual. Lots of things came to mind as possibilities for my feeling sick but a pregnancy was not even remotely one of them. I did not have regular periods and the only man I had been intimate with recently was to my knowledge sterile, so I was concerned that my health condition could be serious.

While having dinner at a close girlfriend's house in Davis, I became extremely nauseated by the ratatouille, one of my favorite foods. My girlfriend had made it knowing how much I loved it. Judith scrutinized me closely and then said, "Your symptoms suspiciously resemble a pregnancy."

"That's crazy," I said. "Albert can't have children. I do not want children. I just started law school. Anyway, it has to be something else."

Unable to eat, I left but not before Judith convinced me to go to a drugstore and buy a pregnancy kit just to make sure. Reluctantly, I agreed to buy a kit on the way home. I could not believe there was even a slight possibility.

Still flushed and feeling ill, I rushed into the drugstore looking around for where the kits might be located. Wandering around for a while, I was mortified to have to ask the store clerk where the pregnancy kits were located. I wondered how it had come to this. Once I located the section, I was in a quandary on the selection since I had no idea which was the best brand. It was too much for me, so I snatched the first package in front of me and rushed toward the cash register.

Once home, I flung the newly purchased kit onto the bathroom sink and headed for bed, not even changing into my night clothes. I was too tired and too sick to deal with any test. I would do it tomorrow. Pulling the covers over my head, I whispered to myself, *I can't be pregnant*, and then fell fitfully asleep.

On waking, my stomach reeled as I dragged myself out of bed, making my way to the bathroom. Seeing the kit lying in the sink, I thought, *let's get this over with* as I started tearing off the packaging. Following the simple instructions, I plopped down on the toilet seat to wait the required two minutes to see what the magic strip revealed. I had no doubt I was not pregnant; but to keep Judith from harassing me, I might as well put this possibility to rest and then figure out what was really wrong.

Daydreaming as I sat on the toilet, I pondered what else could be causing my nausea, letting the two minutes drag to three before I remembered to check. Leaping up, I saw a blue strip which meant I was pregnant. *That's ridiculous*, I uttered to myself

I should have bought more kits. I had read that the blue dye tests are notorious for false positives. *Now I have to go buy another one.*

I had a 10:00 am class, so I decided to stop off at the drugstore on my way home. My stomach was still queasy. Obviously, the ratatouille my girlfriend had served the night before was still messing with my stomach. This time I knew exactly where to go. I grabbed one kit and then a second one for good measure. I was going to prove Judith wrong, and I would not be taking any more chances with false readings.

It was not until later that night that I remembered I had to retest. I had left both kits in my car trunk. After retrieving them, I settled down in the bathroom to redo the test. This time I meticulously watched the time, guessing the first wrong reading was due to my failure to follow the directions carefully. On the two-minute mark, I scrutinized the strip and saw to my dismay another positive reading. Disappointed and frustrated, I ripped open the next kit and redid the test. Only this time I would be more thorough with each step. The results were the same: *pregnant*.

I was beside myself. This could not be possible. I could not have a child now. I grabbed my phone to make an appointment with my doctor later in the week, and then remembered it was late. Calling early the next morning I requested a pregnancy test. Nervous for the next couple of days until I could get to my appointment, I had to keep reminding myself to calm down and wait until after my medical exam before panicking. Surely, there was some explanation; the doctor could sort it out. Maybe it was a tumor? But did tumors cause positive pregnancy readings? It was possible. I was entirely ignorant about this stuff since it had never been on my radar.

I told no one other than Judith. I was not sure what was wrong, but I was really worried. I could not afford to be so distracted from my schoolwork. Finally, the appointment day arrived. I had promised Judith I would give her a call as soon as I left the doctor's office. I described the three positive tests and my boyfriend's previous medical conditions, though I did not know what he would now be called. I explained that in addition to being sterile, the potential father was much older, which made the idea of a pregnancy even more unlikely. I wanted the doctor to know that I had not been intimate with anyone else and that I had never had regular periods, so I was not even sure I could get pregnant. No need to go into the other complicating factors. The doctor smiled as all this information poured out of me in a single breath.

The doctor did a quick physical exam and asked me to provide a urine sample as well. He left the room, returning fifteen minutes later.

His first words on entering were, "It looks like you are pregnant."

Indignant, I asked for another test. The doctor said he would be happy to do another the next day, but he was fairly sure the results would be the same.

"But how is this possible? He is sterile. I thought that could not change and he is much older. Wouldn't that make it even less likely?"

Shaking his head, the doctor said, "Yes, it is unusual. I could consult with his doctor."

"What does the father say?"

Self-conscious, I admitted to the doctor that I had not yet told the father, explaining I had wanted to wait for the results of today's examination. Suddenly, in a burst of exasperation I cried out, "I cannot have a child now. I just entered a strenuous graduate program, and he is… well, his situation is complicated," I ended up, whispering.

The doctor stared at me. *No need to get into the details of what was going on in Albert's life with the doctor,* I thought. "But," I said, "he strongly believes he cannot father children. He had tried for years, and his medical records indicated his low sperm count would never be sufficient."

Laughing, the doctor said, "That may be true, but you are pregnant. So, something happened."

Upset and tearful, I asked the doctor when he would have the results of the second test.

"Call me tomorrow afternoon and I will confirm your fifth test. But I must warn you, it will show you are pregnant," the doctor stated as he left the exam room.

I left the doctor's office confused, unsettled and in tears, determined that there was still a mistake somewhere. I could not, would not have a child now and Albert had already moved on. All this was making it impossible for me to concentrate on my studies.

The following afternoon I got the call I had been waiting for and dreading. My doctor confirmed I was pregnant, about six weeks along. Shocked, I sat down and cried until I could no longer shed another tear. What a complicated mess. I called Judith and confirmed her initial suspicions were correct. Concerned, Judith asked me what I was going to do.

"I honestly don't know," I stammered, "but I have to make up my mind soon."

"Did you tell Albert?" queried Judith.

"No, I'm afraid of how he will take it. Remember, he just moved in with Ann."

"But didn't you tell me he had wanted children?"

Sighing, I said, "Yes, but with those other girlfriends, not me."

"I have to call him and break the news. I am scared of his

response and frankly I don't really know what I am going to do. I am leaning toward an abortion. I never planned on being a mother."

"What are you going to do about school if you go ahead with the pregnancy?" probed Judith.

"Judith, stop with the questions," I cried. "I don't know what to do. I never thought I'd find myself in this kind of situation. I am not even sure I could be a good mother and the circumstances surrounding this pregnancy are beyond problematical."

No one was more surprised than I about the pregnancy, except Albert's mother, who, when later told of the pregnancy, said, "No, It's not possible. Albert can't have children." She went on to explain that the family doctor had told her he was sterile due to an early childhood illness and later again when he got the mumps as a young adult. Albert had always wanted children but had given up hope years earlier.

Chapter 17
The Dreaded Phone Call

I intentionally let more days elapse before getting the courage to call Albert. In fact, I was out at dinner with my friends at a local Mexican restaurant in Jack London Square when I mentioned "the situation" to them and my dilemma about what to do. Their response was outrage that I hadn't told Albert yet. In unison, they demanded I leave the table and call him. "He needs to know he's going to be a father." That is so unfair. Call him now," they shouted together, causing other restaurant patrons to turn and stare.

Pressured, I said, "Okay. I'll call him now. But I must tell you I'm not sure how he'll react."

I excused myself from the margaritas and the scattered tortilla chips covering the table and headed for the pay phones in the back of the restaurant. Taking a deep breath before dialing Albert's number, I wondered what he would say. He answered immediately. I wasn't sure where to start, so I paused for a moment and then nervously said, "I've got some news for you." He waited for me to continue. "I'm pregnant," I gasped.

"Oh, congratulations, Yolanda! I didn't really know you were seeing anyone."

Offended, I exclaimed, "Albert, you are the father!"

"Yolanda, you must be mistaken. You know I cannot have children. It is not mine. I'm not sure I appreciate your saying it is my child."

I shouted into the phone, "Albert, have you ever known me to lie, especially about something like this? I will be happy to take the DNA test to prove it if you need it."

There was a long silence at the other end. "Albert, are you still there?"

"Yes, but I don't understand this. Are you sure you are pregnant?" he asked, dumbfounded by the news he had been given. He was not certain he believed it, much less how he should respond.

"Of course, I'm sure. I took three pregnancy tests and I have my doctor's confirmation," I sputtered.

"But you just started school. What are you going to do?"

"I don't know. This is too upsetting and bad timing," I said, trying to stifle a sob.

Albert was at a total loss for words. If I was pregnant, it meant he would finally be a father. On the other front, it was really bad for his current relationship. I imagined that he had no idea how any of this could be negotiated if I went through with the pregnancy. He remained silent and then said he had to go, quickly hanging up to my dismay.

I returned to my friends, distressed and upset. "What happened?" they asked. I quietly repeated my conversation with Albert. My eyes teared as I realized how incredibly difficult the situation was. My friends remained silent for a couple of minutes, but then quickly regained their composure and told me it would work out. They were the ones who insisted I call him. They looked around the table at each other, secretly making a pact to support me no matter what happened; and they did.

Later that night in bed I tossed and turned. I was in a complete uproar over what to do. My mind flooded with all kinds of doubts, concerns, and worries over the impending time limit to make my decision. I could not have a child now and, more importantly, children had not been part of my plan. And yet, the further along I got in my pregnancy, the more bewildered I became about what to do. I had to act. My time was almost up.

Chapter 18
Yes or No

Frantic, after many internal debates and with a heavy heart, I made an appointment for an abortion. It seemed the only available solution to me at the time. I would get the abortion and then return to my neglected studies. I would not tell Albert, because I was not sure what he would say. It was challenging enough to go through with it without any further emotional impediments. I would tell him afterwards. That was cowardly, but I did not know how else to do it since I was so unsure of how he felt.

The following week I drove to the clinic for my scheduled appointment. I was nervous, scared, and unsure but determined to see my appointment through. I had only gone a couple of blocks when my car sputtered and then came to a complete halt. It would not budge. Frightened, I tried to start it, all to no avail. Glancing at my watch I could see the time creeping closer to my scheduled appointment. Impatient drivers were now honking their horns at me because I was blocking the street. Dragging myself out of the car, I put the hood up and moved to the side of the car. I started crying. I knew I would not make my appointment on time. It had been so hard to get the courage to go and now my stupid car had broken down. I stood by the stalled car unsure of what to do. I needed a tow.

Seeing me crying as I stood by my car, a woman driver stopped, walked over, and asked if she could help. By now, I was sobbing as I explained to the kind stranger that I was missing my abortion appointment. Gazing at me, the woman said, "Perhaps, you weren't meant to get an abortion today. But, if you need a ride there, I will take you. Is that you want? Or do you want to go to a gas station to see about your car? Please tell me where I can take you."

Completely rattled by the kind stranger's comments, I decided at that exact moment that my baby was destined, a child so determined to come to me and Albert no matter what the circumstances that I would not go through with the abortion. Thanking the stranger, I asked for a ride to the nearest gas station where I could get assistance for my car and then I called the clinic to tell them I had changed my mind.

Once I had made my decision, I went to see an old boss of mine, Russ Stillwell, whose class I had taken. He was a down-to-earth psychologist, and I was hoping he could reassure me of my decision or least help me sort it out. He had one adopted son and had had lots of problems with that child. When I posed my question about my doubts in proceeding along with the pregnancy, his words had a profound effect on me. He said, "You know, Yolanda, if I hadn't had my son, I would have traveled the world more, I would have had more money, more things but I would not have grown as an individual as I have had to do because of my child. You have to give up your selfishness, at least some of it, and focus on your child; so, I am a better man having been a parent. I can't tell you what to do, but this is what happened to me."

For the next couple of days, I went through all the scenarios in my head that would have to occur for me to have this baby—leave school, get a job, move back to the city I had just left, get books on babies, schedule an appointment with a psychiatrist, inform Albert and let my family know. It was absolutely mind-boggling. I thought Albert should be the first to know since his current situation might be in jeopardy from the news. Meanwhile, my stomach rolled over and over as waves of nausea kept coming.

I knew my family would be shaken, especially since I had vehemently proclaimed since early childhood that I would not have any children and that nothing would change my mind. Shocked would be a more accurate response. My mother would not be happy about my unmarried status, but that was the least of my problems. I needed money to live and had to move. Albert had to be informed.

He had not called me since our last conversation when he had abruptly hung up. I had promised myself to call him but kept putting it off, knowing it would be a difficult conversation. Feeling ill, I decided to put it off for yet another day. What difference did one more day make, anyway?

The words *call Albert* kept reverberating in my head. I kept brushing these thoughts away like bothersome flies. Finally, knowing I had limited time and troubled by my failure to follow up with him, I picked up the phone and dialed his number.

Albert answered with a hesitant, "*Hello*," after I identified myself. Without wavering, I told Albert I was keeping the baby and we had lots to discuss. There was a resounding silence on the other end of the line which I interpreted as displeasure. In reality, Albert was stunned. He said he had to go, and we would talk in a couple of days.

"But, Albert, we need to talk now."

"I can't do it. This is too much for me. I have a lot to think about. I never thought I'd be a father. You have to give me a couple of days. I'll get back to you." He disconnected the call before I could get in another word. Holding the dead phone in my hand, I was not sure what to think. I knew it would be intense for Albert, but he could at least have continued the discussion. *What about my feelings and the stuff I was dealing with as I contemplated keeping the baby? Didn't that count for anything? I guess not*, I thought to myself, distraught with the way the phone call had gone.

A week later I heard that Albert was not well. According to friends he had become mute, completely unable to speak. He had scheduled a doctor's appointment to see what was wrong. *That's silly*, I thought. *I know perfectly well what's wrong with him.* This business of "not speaking" meant we could not sit down and confer on what we would do. Completely frustrated, I returned to school and asked for a year's postponement while I waited to hear from Albert.

Meanwhile, Albert's doctor conferred with my physician because of the unusual circumstances of the pregnancy to determine if it was possible for him to have children. His doctor was adamant when he said, "There is no possible explanation because all the medical indications are that he cannot father a child, especially now at his age."

His doctor also confirmed that Albert was unable to speak. His muteness caused his doctors to believe he might have a serious illness. After numerous tests, the doctors determined Albert had no serious illness but was severely traumatized by the turn of events which had caused him to temporarily lose his ability to speak. They believed he would speak again. Simultaneously, Albert developed a severe case of psoriasis which remained with him for the rest of his life. Within a month's time, he slowly regained the ability to talk.

Chapter 19
The Agreement

Albert asked if I wanted to marry him when it was clear I was carrying his child. I was sure he asked me out of obligation, not love. I answered him with an emphatic "*no*" even though I knew it was not in my best financial interest. Ann knew nothing about it.

Instead, I sat down and drew up a contract which laid out each of our responsibilities in raising our child. I would sit down with him and go over the details to make sure we agreed. My intention was to make it plain to Albert that he had a choice. He could sign the document, or he could walk away, and I would raise our child alone. It would be his decision. Refusing to sign the agreement would relieve Albert of all parental responsibility and rights. I would not hold his decision to walk against him if that turned out to be his wish.

I thought it unlikely Albert would agree to the terms of the ten-page, detailed agreement which focused on broad areas, such as the qualities we would support in our child as it grew, as well as how holidays would be spent together until our child reached adulthood or no longer wanted parental participation. The latter section required the three of us would always celebrate all major holidays together. Surprisingly, Albert agreed to all the terms. He requested that the birth certificate show him as the father and then signed the document. Albert kept his word, honoring every part of the contract; and he did so much more throughout the years proving over and over his commitment to his child.

The only other fear that I had nurtured at the time was that he would not live long enough to see his child fully grown, since he was fourteen years older and would be fifty years old at the time of his daughter's birth.

Albert and I had lots to talk about besides the agreement I had given him. After fully regaining his voice, Albert made it clear that if he were to go forward, he wanted to be an active participant in the baby's development before the actual birth. He asked that I move in with him once I returned from Davis and as it got closer to the birth date. He wanted to be part of the experience of the pregnancy and attend classes with me. There was one minor problem. He was living with his girlfriend, Ann, who was not happy about being booted out of her home. Ann would have to leave temporarily so I could move in for the duration of my pregnancy. This was all too much for Ann, who was infuriated by the situation.

Albert was able to sway Ann's cooperation by explaining it would not be happening immediately. She had a couple of months' reprieve. He also reassured me that he desperately wanted to be part of his child's birth, every minute of it—the before and the after. Ann was convinced my motive for moving in was a ploy to win Albert back. Hearing Ann's concerns gave me one of the few laughs I had during this stressful period. The last thing I wanted was Albert back. Remarkably, Ann would remain close to Vanessa after having spent so much loving time with her in her early formative years.

Chapter 20
The Housing Dilemma

Panic and nervous thoughts overwhelmed me as I considered the countless problems I faced, including how to support myself in the interim period before the baby's birth. Albert had informed me that I was entirely on my own financially until I moved into his place in early November. I needed housing and a job. I had no money and had given up my city job when I left for school. Worried and stressed about my pregnancy, I called my friend Linda to discuss my predicament. She was able to get me a short-term job in San Francisco.

This was a challenging period for me. Albert was living with his girlfriend, Ann. Other former girlfriends were also still in the picture. My situation was trying since I was the one pregnant, and I was not living with him, nor was I a current girlfriend. I was also aware of the of gossip and speculation among Albert's friends, with some taking sides. I ignored the talk as much as I could. Exhausted with the pregnancy and having to figure out my next steps was more than I could bear. I scheduled a counseling appointment, hoping to get some mental relief, a few suggestions on how to cope with the ongoing girlfriend situation, and how to deal with my biggest fear—motherhood.

Finding housing was tough. Rents in Berkeley and El Cerrito were higher than I could afford. Despite scouring the newspapers daily and driving up and down the streets, I could not locate anything in my price range. Desperate, I tried something different. I believed in the power of visualization and creating a reality to meet my needs. Writing down the figure I thought I could afford for rent—$90 a month—with a description of what the new location should have, I waited patiently for a room to become available. I knew full well the rents for single rooms were going for hundreds of dollars more than my limited budget allowed.

I continued to imagine my new home with lots of windows, good light, in a safe neighborhood and costing $90 a month. Soon thereafter, I located a place in Thousand Oaks, a neighborhood in North Berkeley. It was a single room, featuring six large windows overlooking a lush backyard garden. My new room came with kitchen privileges and was at my pictured price. It was perfect. Thanking my guides, I moved into a new home: a lovely three-story old Victorian house run by an eccentric widow who spent her time traveling the world and who was fascinated by my troubles. She couldn't wait to hear the latest developments in my life which were so far removed from her world. The widow enjoyed giving suggestions on how to manage different situations that kept popping up in my life.

I decided my child would enter the world naturally and completely drug-free even though I would be an older first-time mother. I began studiously reading all the literature on raising children, signed up for general classes on childbirth, as well as Lamaze classes. My doctors cautioned me that I might not be able to deliver my child naturally due to my age. I pooh-poohed their warnings and continued studying everything I could on all aspects of pregnancy. I was worried about Albert. Would he be able to attend the Lamaze classes? To play it safe, I asked my good friend Rosie to be my second pregnancy coach. In the meantime, I spent hours in bed worrying and fretting about how it was going to work. When I wasn't working I began sewing handmade blankets for my baby and working on other baby projects in order to distract myself from the numerous issues needing resolution.

In between my sewing projects, I read book after book on raising babies, wanting to be as knowledgeable as possible. I had serious doubts about my ability to successfully mother a child. I wanted to be armed with as much practical information as possible. I continued seeing a psychologist to discuss my concerns and to help firm up my confidence in the mothering area.

Chapter 21
Lamaze Worries

Albert and I went in for the required amniocentesis testing because of my age. We were elated to discover the baby was a girl. We began debating girls' names. I favored Rose, Albert's mother's name, or Carmella, his sister's name. Albert objected to naming his daughter after any living person. We finally settled on Vanessa Annmarie. Both of us were pleased to have a name attached to our growing baby.

Meanwhile, my body kept ballooning into a visibly pregnant person. My mind set continued to be fearful and anxiety-ridden. *How could I be a good mother?* I kept asking myself. *What did I really know about mothering, given my childhood? What about school? How could I manage a small baby? How would I support myself while attending law school and raising a baby?* Frightened, in my heart I knew I was not true mother material. My lingering doubts kept assuring me that I lacked the most basic mothering skills. Afraid to discuss my feelings with others who might not understand, I kept my concerns to myself, continuing my therapy and reading all the books I could on motherhood and children.

As the date for the first Lamaze session drew near, Albert stopped by to explain he had a problem with attending the first class. One of his former girlfriends, not Ann, was planning a big party for his fiftieth birthday. He felt he had no choice but to attend. Angry, but not surprised by this latest development, I was relieved I had a second coach, but hurt that the first class was not a priority for Albert. I told him I was disappointed and mad. Albert responded by saying that he would ask his girlfriend if I could attend the party. *Hell,* I thought, *that was not the point.* I told him in no uncertain terms that we had a more important engagement that day which he was failing to acknowledge. Putting his hands up in frustration, he stormed out the door, leaving me exasperated.

A couple of hours after our heated discussion, I received a personal invitation from the former girlfriend to attend his birthday party. I declined politely while secretly fuming. How dare his old girlfriend confuse the issue even further.

When the big day arrived, I could not hide my excitement. My coach, Rosie, attended class with me. On arrival I reminded myself that even though Albert was not there, he had faithfully attended all the other pregnancy classes, including the one on circumcision, even though we knew the baby was a girl. Albert had fussed that the class was not necessary.

"For god sakes, we are having a girl," Albert ranted. I held my ground saying we had to go in case the doctors were *wrong*. Grudgingly, he went, squirming through the vivid pictures and descriptions and unhappy about having to be present for something he thought was unnecessary.

The day following the birthday bash I got a call from Albert's bookkeeper, Ruth, who had been a guest at the party. She wanted me to know what happened at the gathering. Pushing on before I could get a word in edgewise, Ruth explained that after Albert blew out his birthday candles, he became tearful and then announced he was going to be a father and he was missing the first Lamaze class. His revelation took the birthday crowd by surprise, causing an immediate hush in the room. His friends knew Ann and the girlfriend holding the party. However, neither of them was *pregnant*. They also knew me. It put a damper on the festivities as guests pondered the situation and what to make of it. Ruth went on to explain that Albert gushed on and on about how thrilled he was to finally be a father. She ended by saying she thought I should know what had happened since Albert had missed the Lamaze class. Stunned, I thanked Ruth and suddenly felt a little better about the missed class.

Chapter 22
Baby Qualms

Since my good friend had secured a short-term job in San Francisco for me, my financial fears had been alleviated. But I continued to agonize about how it would all work out. Books were my constant companions as I searched for answers to help assuage my doubts. The progression of my pregnancy heightened my worries. I really had no one to discuss my true trepidations about whether I could be an adequate mother. Most of my friends never gave much thought to this question. Mothering was something they assumed they could do. The people I knew just jumped in, never fretting for a moment about their adequacy to fill the role or so it seems.

Finally, consumed with guilt and worry, I shared my concerns with my sister. She assured me all new mothers had such anxieties and that I would live up to the role as everyone else did. Not entirely convinced, I decided to take her counseling to heart. It gave me some respite, but my anxiety never completely left me. As my time drew nearer, I became more obsessive about doing everything *naturally*. I did not want drugs, an epidural, or any cutting, and I definitely did not want a C-section under any circumstances. I had also decided I wanted pictures taken of the actual birth. It was Albert's job to take them. The pictures were graphic, and I was so proud of them and wanted to show them at the baby shower later held by my family. My mother thought it shameful and asked that I not share them at the shower. Despite her objections I shared them with close friends.

I reminded Albert over and over about the things I wanted and did not want. Finally, he said, "I got it, Yolanda. We won't do any of them." Nonetheless, I continued to worry he would give in to insistent doctors, so I relayed my concerns to my second coach to ensure all would go well and as planned. Finally, to make doubly sure, I made a list of the *"no, no's"* and handed them to Albert on a lined, yellow, legal sheet of paper so he wouldn't forget. Annoyed, he shook his head when he saw the list.

Then, I moved on to the 'party" part of the birth. I wanted to have a big celebration with a cake, champagne, and gifts for my coaches. I ordered a cake that said, 'Welcome Vanessa.' I bought sweatshirts for Albert and Rosie. Albert's said, 'No. 1 Coach,' and Rosie's said, 'No. 2 Coach.'

My bag was packed. I was ready. In fact, I was growing impatient for the birth to occur. I wanted it over. I told my doctor that I would have an early delivery date. Smiling, he assured me that was always possible, just as the baby could arrive a couple of weeks late. He said, "New mothers always want the baby to be early." Ignoring his amusement, I was sure my daughter would be early. Vanessa delivered one week early.

Chapter 23
Panic at the Hospital

Albert and I had gone to the movies that evening. I was not feeling well; but that had been the case for the last couple of weeks, so I dismissed my cramping and uncomfortableness as the status quo until the birth. We got home early and retired to bed. I was awakened by sharp pains around midnight. I looked over at Albert, who was sleeping peacefully, and debated whether to wake him. I decided to let him sleep.

As pain increased, I slipped quietly out of bed and ran to shower. I had read all the books. They were clear that the best way to lessen the early discomfort was to stay in the shower. There was something about the hot water stream hitting your face and body that numbed the pain. I did feel slightly better as the water bombarded me and steamed up the bathroom. Finally, the hot water ran out. Shuddering and prune-skinned, I grabbed a towel and went to wake Albert. I needed to call Rosie, too.

It was now close to 7:00 am and I was starting to panic. I needed to get to the hospital. Rushing, I screamed at Albert to hurry. We had to leave, but there was so much to load in the car because of the planned party. Rosie would meet us at the hospital. As we drove to the Berkeley hospital, it seemed as though Albert was hitting every red light. I convulsed with each new contraction.

"Run the red light," I shouted at Albert. Looking concerned, Albert looked over at me and said, "I can't do that." Gripping the wheel, he said we would make it on time. I was not sure. It felt as though the baby was coming, and we were not even close to the hospital.

On arriving at the hospital, we rushed to the emergency entrance where the waiting attendants placed me in a wheelchair and raced me to the Maternity Ward. Albert lagged behind, weighed down with all the packed items he had to carry in. I knew I was in the second stage of the birthing process because of the level of pain I was experiencing on the way to the hospital. The books had described it as the hardest and most painful part of labor. I had waited too long to leave. I had purposely lingered, wanting to be sure I got into the natural birth labor room. There was only one available at that time, and the mother closest to giving birth got the room.

Still, I was concerned my dilation number was not high enough. I held my breath as I was placed on the examining table. I prayed I would get into the natural birthing center. It was only after I heard the nurse say I was at eight centimeters that I exhaled a full breath. I was close to giving birth. I was thankful but now could not avoid noticing the elevated level of pain wracking my body.

I had said I did not want any medication. I wanted everything to be natural—no medications for my baby or me. It was one of the *absolutely do not do things* on my hospital list. In severe pain, I was rethinking that self-imposed rule. I had been wrong or unwise to think I was above the pain. I now wanted something to lighten the aching. I needed something badly. I asked for aspirin or anything that would help alleviate the hurting. Shaking their heads, the nurses told me it was too late for anything. Too near to giving birth, I would have to bear it. Gritting my teeth, I knew it was my fault I was now in this position.

My daughter was delivered a short while later in the birthing room. She was beautiful as she uttered her first scream, but she was quickly whisked away by the nurses. Albert opened the champagne, handing Rosie and me a glass. He was very emotional. Tears flowed down his cheeks as he started making phone calls to announce his daughter's arrival. We cut the cake, and I gave Albert and Rosie their gifts. Exhausted, I wanted to shower in the bathroom located in the room. After returning refreshed, I saw Albert had fallen asleep in the chair. Rosie was dozing but awake.

There was no sign of the baby. I asked the nurse to bring the baby to me. The nurse looked uneasy and said the doctor would be in soon. Upset and worried why they would not bring the baby in, I started to pace around the small room. Soon after, the doctor walked in and explained that the baby was in the ICU. "Why? Why?" Albert and I cried, demanding an explanation. Shaking his head, the doctor said they noticed the baby was born with a cleft palate. Cleft palates are formed in the eleventh week in the womb. Vanessa's cleft palate opening was large and only partially formed. The doctors decided to force feed her to see if she could eat, because they would not release her if she was unable to eat. This procedure caused her to stop breathing, resulting in Vanessa being placed in the ICU.

I had read enough to know that babies didn't have to eat for several hours after birth. "Why was she fed? She didn't need to eat immediately," I kept asking the doctors. To my consternation, my question was ignored. Hysterical at this point, I insisted on going to the ICU immediately to see our baby. The nurses led the way to the ICU with Albert and me trailing close behind. Staring at our newborn in her warmer bed, I started crying. Albert reached for my hand. He was clearly shaken, too. The nurses rushed us out of the ICU and told us the doctor wanted to meet us back in the birthing room to discuss the situation.

Reluctantly, we left our daughter in the ICU. Back in the room, a nurse entered and informed me that I would be released later that day. Furious, I told her to inform the doctors that I would not leave my daughter in the hospital alone. I insisted on remaining in the hospital until my daughter was discharged. The hospital was not happy with my decision but agreed to transfer me to a hospital room later that evening. I remembered my earlier hospital experience, and that memory required that I protect my daughter, no matter what.

Shortly thereafter, the doctor returned. He began explaining that cleft palates are a birth defect which are often genetically inherited. However, neither Albert's nor my family had any such history. We shared this information with the doctor. The doctor went on to say there could be many causes, including stress, age, etc., I stopped carrying on when I heard this because I recalled how stressed I had been for most of my pregnancy. Perhaps it was my fault or it happened because of our ages, although Albert was older. We were told we had to have follow-up genetic testing. We tried to explain there would be no further children, but it was still required.

The doctors went on to warn Albert and me there could be numerous medical issues affecting our daughter, from ear problems, to eating issues to chances of choking and speech impediments. The cautions went on and on until I refused to listen any further. I did not want to hear these possibilities. I was not even sure their warnings would all happen. I would sign up for a class on cleft palates after leaving the hospital and find out all I could. I had to discover what had caused the problem. Afraid, I believed I might be the reason. I wanted to make sure I knew everything about the potential side effects that might affect our baby. I was going to make damn sure my daughter was not touched by all the ailments the doctors said impacted cleft palate children.

I later took a class at Sonoma State University on cleft palates and the latest research. The class was clear that there could be multiple causes other than genetics and that it was often impossible to determine one single cause. Now I understood why mandatory genetic counseling was required. I still feared that my extreme stress may have caused my daughter's problem. Albert and I were committed to doing everything to ensure our daughter had the best health care and speech therapy possible.

Chapter 24
Feeding Troubles

Two days later my daughter and I were released from the hospital. Albert picked us up. I had planned on breast-feeding, but no specific feeding instructions were given to us as new parents. We were both so overjoyed to be leaving the hospital with our newborn daughter that it did not occur to us to ask about feeding her. We knew little of cleft palate situations. Staring down at my precious daughter, I couldn't believe I had almost missed my chance to meet her.

Tired but happy to be home, I lovingly placed the baby in the crib. Ruth had knitted a beautiful baby blanket which was lightly placed over Vanessa. Albert and I stood by the crib gazing at our daughter. We both decided that for the first couple of months the baby would be in our room in a bassinet by the bed because of all the warnings of possible chokings the doctors had showered on us. We were well aware of SID deaths and did not want to risk our daughter's life by failing to monitor her closely.

My friends, as promised, came to the house after Vanessa's birth, volunteering to help clean, do the laundry and watch the baby while I caught up with sleep. My second coach, Rosie, made it her business to sleep over so she could get up in the middle of the night to take care of Vanessa's feedings. This support helped alleviate some of my anxiety about her care and feeding. Their kindness was deeply appreciated.

At birth, Vanessa weighed seven pounds and fourteen ounces. The doctors had explained that babies lose a small amount of weight after being discharged from the hospital, though they quickly gain it back as they continue to grow. Albert returned to work. I tried to breast-feed Vanessa for the first couple of days unsuccessfully. It was unclear if she was getting any food at all, so we tried using a bottle with expressed milk. We tried everything. Vanessa spent lots of time crying, and soon I was crying along with her, despairing over my inability to feed her. Albert would return home to find us both weeping. I was disturbed that Vanessa was losing weight because she was not eating. I spent hours trying to feed her and could not get her to eat. Nothing seemed to work. I did not want her to go back to the hospital.

Her weight loss was confirmed at the first checkup a couple of days after her release. At the visit, the doctors strongly warned that if Vanessa's weight fell any further or to five pounds she would be hospitalized. Nothing seemed to work. Albert and I were worried sick about Vanessa's inability to eat. Desperate, I called everyone, asking how to feed my daughter. The hospital was not much help.

It was not until I located a breast-feeding organization who agreed to do a home visit that we finally got the information we needed to properly feed Vanessa. They explained my daughter could not breast-feed because she did not have sufficient palate closure to draw the milk into her mouth. The open cleft palate prevented suction. This meant she also could not drink milk from a regular bottle. Because of the sizable opening in her palate, any liquids she drank would directly leak out of her nose or pool in her mouth, causing a choking reaction. Choking was a strong possibility, so great care needed to be taken to ensure she was suctioned if there was any gagging response.

Requesting a regular bottle nipple, the volunteer took out a sharp razor blade, and proceeded to cut a large diagonal and a horizontal slash across the top. The result was that the nipple was completely open. She explained the baby could now get adequate milk into her mouth. We would still have to be careful about choking, though, because lots of milk would spill through the gashed nipple. When the bottle with the newly cut nipple was placed into Vanessa's mouth, there was a small gasp. She slowly started swallowing substantial amounts of milk, causing some of it to flow directly out of her nose. It was clear she was hungry. I was ecstatic. My daughter could now

THE SACRED VOW

eat and gain back the lost weight. Though saddened that I could not breast-feed, I was happy we were finally on the right track. Vanessa started gaining weight in the next couple of weeks as she sipped from her new bottle.

The doctors at the hospital had explained that our daughter would need several surgeries to correct the cleft palate. They recommended the first one to be at fifteen months. That seemed so far away. I tried not to think about it. The good news was that Vanessa had an entire panel of different medical specialists who would help determine when to schedule the needed surgeries. Their focus would be on what was best for Vanessa. She had five surgeries to correct her palate situation.

Chapter 25
Return to School and Vanessa's First Surgery

I had to return to school because my leave of absence was up in August. Albert and I would co-parent our daughter. This meant Vanessa would live with her dad during the week to be close to her doctors and then with me on weekends. It wasn't the best plan, but it was the only one that we thought would work. I felt terribly guilty leaving my child who was eight months old to return to school. I had read that hearing a mother's voice was imperative for development in the early months. I called often during the week to speak to my daughter. Albert would place the phone next to Vanessa's ear so she could hear my voice. I wasn't sure if this helped, but I wanted to establish a loving bond with my new daughter. I was afraid we wouldn't bond properly.

I also sent letters to my daughter and asked Albert to read them to her. I had trouble concentrating on my studies. When fellow women students asked if I had any children, I would explain I had a daughter who lived with her father. I couldn't help noticing their surprised looks. Their reaction saddened me and added to my guilt at not being physically present in Vanessa's everyday life. Sometimes I explained the medical reasons, but at other times I did not.

We soon fell into a routine where I would drive down Friday evening to El Cerrito to pick up my daughter and then drive back. It was often late because I had to finish my job before leaving. Sometimes Albert would bring her to Davis and then I would drive her back.

Summers in Davis were often ridiculously hot. When returning home with Vanessa from her dad's on late Sunday afternoons, I made sure to keep a water spray bottle in the car to cool her off. Even with the air conditioner at the highest setting Vanessa's cheeks would flush a bright red from the heat. Frightened and afraid she might suffer a heatstroke, I made it a habit to spray water on her sweet face, hoping to cool her down. It meant I had to keep taking my eyes off the road because the car seat was in the back, but I had no choice.

Trying to study, work and travel back and forth drained me tremendously. I was constantly worried about my daughter and my grades, and I was barely managing to hold on. We had agreed that after Vanessa's first surgery, she would live permanently with me in Davis.

Vanessa's first surgery was scheduled in August, right after she turned fifteen months old. The doctors advised us that both of her arms would be encased in plaster casts to prevent her from touching her mouth after the surgery. She would be staying in the hospital for several days. This news triggered all my old fears about hospitals and my daughter's safety while there. I advised Albert that I would not allow Vanessa to remain in the hospital unchaperoned even for a brief time. We would have to be at the hospital twenty-four hours watching over her until she was released. This meant that Albert, Ann, his current girlfriend, and I would each do separate hospital shifts. I was surprised that Ann had volunteered to help, but was grateful. I wanted someone with my daughter at all times.

It was painful seeing my young daughter standing up in the hospital crib with plaster casts on both arms. She looked so vulnerable, and she cried because she couldn't bend her arms. I was a mess, as was her dad. I was worried about the surgery, which would be the doctor's first attempt to close as much of the upper palate as possible. It would be difficult because there was hardly any soft palate available to close the open space. The soft palate had to be pulled towards the center bridge and then sewn to it. Since this part of the palate is very thin the doctors worried it would tear and not stay attached to the bridge.

THE SACRED VOW

Leaving a large opening in the roof of her small mouth could cause eating, sleeping and speech impediments. Little Vanessa was just beginning to say a few words, which had a deep husky tone to them due to the lack of closure of the upper palate. Her doctors made sure we both knew the surgery might not be successful since there was so little tissue to work with. They also said she would need speech therapy as she grew older.

On the day of the surgery, Albert, Ann, and I huddled together nervously in the reception area waiting to hear from the doctors. After several hours, her doctors reported the surgery went well; but it would take a couple of days to see if it would hold since the tissue was so fragile. During that time, Vanessa contracted a staph infection. The surgery was unsuccessful. All the suffering my daughter had endured, including the casts, and then it didn't work. We were devastated, even though the doctors said future surgeries could still correct the problem.

Vanessa had five surgeries in total, some more frightening than others in an attempt to close the palate opening. One surgery required that a thin layer of tongue tissue be thinly sliced and then sewn to the top of the roof of her mouth. The doctors were hoping that tougher tongue tissue would adhere better than the softer palate tissue. This procedure required that her jaw be wired shut for six weeks while the healing process occurred. All her food had to be pureed in order for her to sip the liquids through a straw. Her dad spent hours liquifying all types of foods, including hot dogs, so that she could taste familiar foods. This surgery closed the hole a little more, but an opening still remained.

The doctor's next attempt was to create a pharyngeal flap which they said would help her speech and sound reverberate properly. Doctors advised this procedure could cause headaches and snoring. We both decided speech therapy should begin early so that Vanessa would learn proper tongue placement for speech. Albert and I went ahead and scheduled an orthodontic appointment so that monitoring could occur from an early age. She was two years old when she began speech therapy.

Cleft palate children are born with small jaws. The final surgery, which I opposed, was at age sixteen. Vanessa's jaw would be broken, wired shut again so her jaw could be properly realigned. Several teeth would also be removed at the same time. I saw it as cosmetic, but Vanessa and her dad wanted it to be done; so, I acquiesced knowing it would be the last one. It was successful but it was a hard six weeks of liquefying all types of food which had to be sipped through a straw.

We had always stayed with Vanessa in the hospital for each surgery. She was sixteen when the last surgery was scheduled. Vanessa advised us we did not need us to stay with her. I was worried but wanted to honor her need to do it alone, so we agreed. The day after her surgery we found out there had been a problem overnight and that Vanessa had been moved to the ICU. She asked that we stay with her for the remaining hospital visit. The surgery was successful.

Chapter 26
Law School

I worked and did internships while in law school. One job I had was for the Assistant Public Defender in Yolo County. I was excited to learn about how the criminal system worked for those lacking the resources to hire private attorneys. Though I really admired those laboring in this section of the criminal justice system, I found it alarming when working in it up close. My boss, Lou, was diligent but could not keep up with the huge caseload. After working for a couple of weeks, I marched into court with him carrying piles of files. He had files too. Men in orange suits were waiting in a long single line. Lou pointed to the first one and said "guilty," and the second one, "not guilty"—and on and on it went. I was dismayed. Leaving, I asked him if he had looked at the files. He shrugged, saying he didn't have time. It was then I knew I wanted nothing to do with the criminal justice system and its overworked staff.

On occasion, I was sent to court to observe conservatorship hearings in order to learn how to represent clients initiating such actions. People would say cruel things in court in front of close relatives to support their request for a conservatorship over their relatives' or spouses' property. It was upsetting to see families grapple with their loved ones' financial holdings.

Each day brought more complaints of abused minors. It was disturbing to read repeated case histories of abused children with no immediate solution in sight. Fortunately, I was not assigned to any cases involving minors.

The final blow came one day when I was asked to enter a private investigation room and assist an interrogator who spoke no Spanish.

I had made it clear when I was hired that I did not speak fluent Spanish. I had explained I could understand some general words and conversations. That day the regular interpreter was unavailable, so my supervisor insisted I help. The interrogators were desperate to get several questions answered. Protesting, I said it would not be fair to the man because I did not have an adequate vocabulary nor was I familiar with the legal terms that might be part of the conversation. They wanted me to try it, anyway. I entered the room reluctantly and worried.

The gentleman being interviewed had murdered someone. He started describing how he had stabbed the victim, and the question from the interrogator was, "What type of knife had he used?" I panicked because I couldn't recall the word for knife in Spanish. All that came to my mind was the word for fork. It truly frightened me that this man's future might be jeopardized even more by an incompetent interpreter. I got up and left the room saying I couldn't interpret properly. I was really upset. A short while later I decided to find another job.

After leaving the Public Defender's Office, I got a job working for Yolo County Mental Health as an advocate for those wishing to be released from a psychiatric facility after being on a 5150 (72-Hour Mental Health Involuntary Hold). I was attracted to mental health issues, and it is one of the reasons I had elected to go to law school. I wanted to work with the mentally ill.

I learned a lot in my new job, but the most profound thing I would take away was that mental illness is not an all-encompassing state of mind. An individual could be perfectly sane in all other areas of their life and still be classified as mentally ill. I saw this situation over and over as I worked with a wide variety of mental health patients.

The patients I represented were held in different locked facilities, including Napa State Hospital. My role was to secure their release if that is what they wanted when their temporary hold was up after 72 hours. I would appear in front of an administrative law judge and present an argument on why the patient should be released. I had to prove these persons were not a danger to themselves or others, and that they could provide food and shelter for themselves.

I took to advocacy and was remarkably successful in getting my patients released. This achievement did not endear me to the psychiatrists. It got to the point where they were complaining I was getting too many patients released. I was surprised and angered, since that was my job or wasn't it? After working at the County for a while, I was warned by the administrative law judge I appeared in front of regularly that the head psychiatrist wanted me terminated.

It was at this time that I came to believe that the most dangerous people in the mental facilities were not patients but the psychiatrists. Mind you, not all of them; but many of them wanted to hold on to patients indefinitely and continue to medicate them. Some of my cases caused them grief because they did not want to release their patients, even though a legal determination had been made that the person no longer needed to be held involuntarily.

I spent lots of time in locked facilities and was never afraid of the patients except on two occasions. One time a patient at Napa State Hospital rushed into our hearing room wielding a knife. Luckily, he ran back out. We locked the door after he exited. The other time was when I looked into a patient's eyes, and I had to step back as fear gripped my throat. I left rather than talk to her. I knew right away that I couldn't help her.

I had many unusual cases and read devastating mental health records that would bring most people to tears. The two cases that most outraged my bosses were quite interesting because they represented society's ways of thinking and conforming. Both patients had mental issues but were able to carve out a way of surviving despite their illness.

The first was a brilliant woman with her PhD who believed cars emitted toxic fumes (a common theme for the mentally ill). In order to protect herself she wore plastic covering all over her body, including her arms and legs. Only her face was uncovered. The plastic caused skin issues because her skin could not breathe, but that is not why she kept getting arrested and confined to mental facilities. She chose to wear transparent plastic and because it generated lots of heat she wore nothing underneath it, which caused problems in public. She had been arrested numerous times for indecent exposure. If I didn't get her out this time she was headed for a commitment in a long-term facility.

When we met I explained to her she could not risk another arrest—she had to change. I thought if I could convince her to wear opaque plastic I could get her out. It took some talking but she was able to process the consequence of not changing her behavior, so she reluctantly agreed. I told her I would need her to make a commitment in front of the judge that she would never wear transparent plastic again.

On the hearing date, I was nervous. Could I convince the judge that opaque plastic would work? No plastic would be best, but that was not an option for her given her fear of fumes. I decided humor might help my argument. She calmly explained to the judge that she would no longer wear transparent plastic but that she could not give up plastic coverings entirely because of the dangerous fumes. I then chimed in, "You know, many people use plastic in the privacy of their homes and bedrooms for a variety of reasons, and no one questions that." The judge raised an eyebrow and tried to refrain from laughing out loud. She was released to my delight and against her doctor's objections.

The second case involved a man who didn't want to live in a regular house. He had constructed his home out of chicken wire, had insulated it and put cardboard all around to make it cozy. He had set up electricity somehow and was quite happy with his tiny home. However, the doctors said he could not live there, and living there proved he had mental issues.

When I met with him I tried to understand why he wanted to live there. He described his place with such pride, as he had built it with little cost. He had limited resources for housing so he was happy there, and he could not understand why he was locked up for choosing a housing situation that worked for him. I knew I would have to convince the judge that we each are entitled to select our own housing and that no one has to conform to society's standards. So, I argued that if he was warm and could sustain himself there, then he should be permitted to have his housing choice, although it might not be the kind others would select. "Do we have a right to choose for him?" I asked the judge. The judge agreed with me, and he was released.

This was the case that got me into trouble. I'm not sure the County wanted a real patient advocate. I suspect they wanted someone who represented the status quo, and who would go along with the psychiatrists' recommendations. I decided that could not be me, so I resigned before they could terminate me.

Chapter 27
Shared Custody

I finished the first year of law school and started making plans for Vanessa to join me in Davis. I soon realized that my daughter might need to stay with her father to be closer to her doctors since more surgeries were planned. The idea that she would not be with me was overwhelming. We both decided it would be best for her to be with me. I hired someone to look after her while I attended school, and she moved to Davis with me. It meant Vanessa would be spending the weekends with her father and weekdays with me.

It was difficult attending law school, working and raising a small child. I could study but was easily distracted by my daughter, who needed my attention when I was home. I struggled with the daily tasks of cooking and managing a home. One day I noticed we were out of milk and didn't know when I could get it the next day, so I waited for Vanessa to fall asleep. I then left the apartment through the sliding patio door, since opening the front door would have awakened her and alerted her I had left. I closed the door but did not lock it. My plan was to run to a nearby store, get the milk and rush right back. I thought I was being careful. The door was too heavy for her to open.

On returning and entering my parking spot, I saw a crowd had gathered and I heard crying that sounded suspiciously like Vanessa. Jumping out of the car and running toward the group, I saw a woman holding a crying Vanessa. The woman looked up at me and asked where I had been in a sharp tone. I held up the milk, but she continued, "Don't you know how dangerous it is to leave a small child at home alone?"

"She was asleep," I countered, "and I didn't believe she had the strength to open the heavy sliding door. She had never done it before." The woman handed Vanessa over to me. Her disapproval was obvious. I was crestfallen and terrified that one of them would call and report me and I would lose my daughter. I rushed into the apartment, hugging my daughter, and crying right along with her. I never left her unattended again.

We got into a routine, shuffling Vanessa back and forth. I was the fussier of the two parents. Albert was more laid back and less concerned with his daughter's appearance. I had Vanessa's clothes made and took great pains to make sure my daughter was clean and dressed well before her dad picked her up. Albert would return her with mismatched clothes and a dirty face. When questioned about where her other clothes were, he'd claim he had no idea. To me, my daughter returned looking like an orphan. Quarreling with Albert did no good. He'd simply laugh and say clothes were unimportant and a little dirt was safe for children. He had a theory that germ exposure was good. Often I'd watch Albert kneeling down in front of Vanessa, trying to wash her face before entering the house. He'd pull out a kerchief, spit into it and then commence cleaning her face. This upset me but I pretended I had not seen what was happening right outside my front door.

With more surgeries coming up, we switched our schedule when Vanessa was three. Vanessa would spend weekdays with Albert and weekends with me. I would drive down Friday afternoons to pick up my daughter each week. On one occasion, I arrived to find Vanessa's arm in a cast. Hysterical, I asked Albert what had happened.

Why hadn't he told me? He calmly explained that Vanessa had fallen from the monkey bars at the day care playground and broken her arm. "I didn't see the point in calling and upsetting you. There was nothing you could do about it there anyway. It was just a break," he said nonchalantly. "Children break bones. It's no big deal."

Speechless and furious, I couldn't understand why Albert hadn't notified me. He didn't even see that it was important that I knew what was happening with my daughter. There was nothing I could do now. Vanessa seemed fine and was proud of the signatures and pictures on her cast. I knew I had to figure out a way to get my daughter back to Davis with me.

Albert would take Vanessa to his favorite bar, and they would give her a Shirley Temple. When I found often about these trips I warned him I did not want her in bars. She was a young child, and it was illegal. Albert denied taking her there, but her hair always gave her away. A whiff of cigarette smoke lingered in her hair. Albert didn't smoke. It was upsetting, but I could tell Vanessa loved going there, sitting on the bar stool and being the center of attention. The Shirley Temple had won her over and though I threatened Albert I believe he continued to take her there.

The weekend trips were hard on all of us. On one trip home with Vanessa, I was stopped by the highway patrol on Highway 80. It was late and I was exhausted. I was having trouble staying in my own lane, though I tried. Soon, I saw flashing blue lights behind me. Upset, I pulled over. The last thing I needed was a ticket. The officer asked me if I had been drinking. I laughed. *If only it was that easy*, I thought. The flashing blue lights woke up Vanessa and she let out a cry. It was then the officer shown his flashlight on her face in the back seat.

"Get off at the next stop and get coffee. I am following you there," he said kindly, lowering his voice now that he had seen my child in the backseat.

Sighing and yet relieved I did not get a ticket, I stopped and got the coffee. He drove away as soon as my car pulled into the takeout line. "One large black coffee," I said to the machine. Vanessa kept saying, "Mommy, mommy, what happened? Why did we get stopped?" Reassuring my daughter, I said, "Oh, sweetie, I wasn't driving as straight as I should, so he stopped me to make sure we were safe. Wasn't that nice?" Mollified, Vanessa accepted my explanation.

I worked hard and completed the next two years of school with Vanessa with me. I moved back to the Bay Area and rented Albert's house. My sister and I moved in, along with Vanessa. Shortly thereafter, we had to move again. The house had been sold so Albert could buy a nearby house.

Chapter 28
Bar Exam

Finally finished with law school, I was so thrilled to get out. It had not been an enjoyable experience though I liked school environments. I had a job offer waiting with a mental health advocacy group pending passing the bar exam. Scared and worried, I studied hard. The bar exam is a two-day process. Purses were not allowed in the exam room. Women were advised to bring a small, translucent, plastic cosmetic bag or something where the entire contents could be viewed. This meant leaving my wallet home and just carrying my driver's license.

On the scheduled day, I drove to Sacramento where the exam was being held. As I sped along the Highway 80 causeway my car sputtered and then came to a complete stop. Panicked, I knew you could not enter the exam late. I looked around for help. I would have to hitchhike the rest of the way to make the exam in time. I left a note on my car that said, "Please, only tow to the nearest gas station. I am in an exam. I will be back before 6 pm." As I jumped into a stranger's car completely frazzled, I prayed my car would be at the closest gas station when I returned.

Arriving just minutes before the exam started, I was shaken and worried about my car. Adrenaline poured through my body as I sat down to start the exam. I had trouble concentrating. I answered the questions and hoped my responses were good enough to pass. I would have to return the next day for the second part of the exam.

Afterwards, I got a ride from a fellow exam taker to the closest gas station. My car was not there. It took me a while to find out that it had been towed to a city garage in Sacramento. I called and told the attendants I couldn't get my car that day. I would have to come the next day. They said, "Fine, there is a daily fee plus towing charges which will be due when you pick it up. You have to pay cash." I saw no point in picking up the car that day since it didn't run, and I didn't have that kind of cash on me. I borrowed a car for the next day's half-day exam. Afterwards, I made my way to the garage to arrange having my car towed back to El Cerrito.

The exam results were out in a month. I failed. I was not surprised. Everyone tried to reassure me that lots of people failed the first time, and you simply would retake the exam as many times as needed to pass. The pending job offer was rescinded. The advocacy group did say they would reconsider my employment once I passed the bar exam. Friends who failed scheduled a retake. I thought long and hard about it, and decided I wouldn't do it.

I had initially decided to go to law school to make the world a little better with a fervent desire to work in mental health facilities. While in law school and through my internships, I discovered that the law wasn't as much about justice and righting the wrongs in the world as it was about maintaining the status quo. Though I completed my law degree. I decided that a career in law was not for me. I couldn't save the world. I was worried about saving myself.

Though I never did practice law officially, I was able to use my training in subsequent positions throughout my career. Perhaps, my stalled car was a sign to reconsider my planned path.

Chapter 29
Raising Vanessa

After finishing law school it was decided I would move in with Albert temporarily until I could get my own place. I had doubts about it and Albert, too, was cautious. I was confused about what I expected, and this is where a serious misunderstanding about our relationship began. Ann was no longer in the picture. To outsiders we were a couple, though it was mostly a fantasy. Albert was involved in his many activities, including regular hunting excursions. He was seeing other women, unbeknownst to me. I thought we were in a relationship, but I was not sure just what type it was. He had mixed feelings about my presence in his home. He felt he was helping me get on my feet and he liked having his daughter nearby.

Albert's attorney held a strong suspicion that I was after his resources and consequently was always having me sign documents declaring I had no interest in his stock purchases, partnership agreements and various other business documents. These requests were insulting, but I signed them anyway. Albert would laugh and say his attorney did not trust me. I thought this suspicion was silly. If I had wanted Albert's money, I would have married him. I knew that much. But the signing of documents continued through the years until I left Albert's house for the final time.

For some odd reason, the relationship bumbled along with Vanessa starting school, and we continued acting like regular parents raising a daughter. It was confusing to teachers and others. When I had to send notes or sign report cards for Vanessa, I would sign my name and then write out the word "mother" in parenthesis since

Vanessa's last name was different than mine. It took some explaining to people who asked, too. People saw Albert and me as a couple; but Albert was pursuing other relationships and I was pretending we were a couple. In some ways, we were, and in other ways we were not. I preferred being forthright and wanted to explain that Albert and I were not married. The rest of our situation was too difficult to clarify.

Lots of people, including Vanessa's teachers, thought our relationship was unusual. Though not married, we were not bitter or unfriendly towards each other. Albert and I were friends as we had been so for many years before our relationship changed. We routinely gave each other gifts on all occasions, even in the worst of times. We were committed to raising our daughter together. I secretly wanted more. It was unclear if Albert knew this, but he continued seeing other women and on occasion we fought about it. He did not see our relationship in the same way I did.

Albert always presented me to others, saying, "This is Vanessa's mother." I learned to ignore the looks that appeared on people's faces when I was introduced to new people. It was okay. I never regretted my decision not to marry. It was a commitment I had made to myself.

Albert and I remained together while Vanessa was in elementary school. Our bond concerned raising our daughter and doing everything we could to help with her scheduled medical procedures. We were partners, not lovers. I was still interested in the relationship, but he was pursuing other interests and women. Lost and confused this was a difficult period for me.

In the meantime, my boss continued making overtures. Concerned I told Albert I was worried about how to manage the situation. He dismissed my worries as figments of my imagination.

I put on a brave face and kept hoping things would change. Over time it became clear that Albert's romantic interests lie elsewhere. Meanwhile my boss's interest lit a little flame of hope that there was someone who did care and who thought I was worthy of time and love.

Chapter 30
The Affair

During my first year of working with Tony, it occurred to me that he had a crush on me. I did not understand why and only thought of him as my "boss." I pretended not to notice his increasing attention. It was simply too awkward and uncomfortable.

We didn't start off as lovers. I respected him as my boss and wanted to maintain a professional relationship. I had had difficulties in the workplace before, so I wanted to be careful. Besides, he was married, much older and I had enough on my plate. I was not looking for romance—just money and a decent job to care for my young daughter.

Our personal relationship would develop very slowly over a long, four-year period. This pace was vastly different from the earlier relationships I had experienced as a young woman. It would be years before we became a couple. I was not easily won over. My daughter's father had waited seven years before I had agreed to even consider expanding our friendship to "something more."

Tony was fourteen years older than me. This age difference was nothing compared to my earlier lover, Ed, who had been thirty years older. In general, I preferred older men. They knew a thing or two about women that often-escaped younger men.

In the beginning, Tony approached me carefully and tentatively, afraid I would brush him off. He had observed that I could be short with men I thought were trying to engage my attention. He must have decided the easiest way to win me over was to spend time conversing with me about subjects that he thought I would find interesting. He made it a point to stop by my office whenever he could without calling too much attention to it. He was the boss and others watched his every move closely. Excessive visits to a new staffer would be noticed by others and discussed by all, causing widespread gossip.

At times, he would invite me to his office. He would ask me questions about my current assignments, often keeping me there after my scheduled work hours. Although I had a thirty-mile commute home, I didn't really mind because we discussed a variety of topics, many which were new to me and of special interest. This delay caused me to pick up my daughter late on more than one occasion, which should have been a red flag.

We often had lunch together with his assistant, and at times we were joined by other management staff. These luncheons were extremely uncomfortable for me. I had to make conversation, and I was definitely not up to their level. In the early days, I felt so insecure and shy that I remained mostly silent at these outings. As I grew more comfortable, I shared limited pieces of personal information about my life and my daughter. But I was inclined to be secretive about my situation and my life in general. If the others noticed, they were too polite to say anything or point it out. They did not seem surprised by my reticence to speak at the weekly luncheons.

It was Tony's self-effacement I noticed first, and it is what I admired about him. It was an unusual quality in a man, a trait I secretly admire in people and one I valued in him. I was used to men with overly confident personalities, sure of themselves and their placement in the world. He was not like that.

Tony was a romantic. He wrote voluminous love letters to me, sometimes two a week, which he mailed to me. His letters declared his love and devotion. At times, I thought they were a little over the top, but I enjoyed receiving them and was always delighted when a new one showed up in my mailbox. I've kept all of Tony's letters and when nostalgic I pull them out and read them.

He knew of my wish to travel, so he encouraged me to venture out further than I had ever before. We often talked about trips he had taken and exciting places in the world to visit. He knew I wanted to visit Greece with my close girlfriend. He offered to pay for my trip to Greece to celebrate my birthday. I thought hard about the appropriateness of accepting such a gift, although at this point we had been in a relationship for many years. I decided to accept the birthday gift. The night before the trip, he came by to watch me pack. He was as excited about the trip as I was. He had traveled the world, so he knew the adventures I would experience.

Tossing my favorite short, yellow, rayon dress with grey flowers into my suitcase, I saw Tony pull it out of the suitcase and place it on the bed. "You can't take that dress; it's too short and not right for the trip," he said frowning. Smiling, I asked him why he didn't want me to take it. It was at that moment I saw a determined look I knew so well. It wasn't worth arguing about, but I was not so easily deterred. When he got distracted, I plucked it from the bed and quickly repacked it. I hid it under other items when he was not looking. He was happy I left the dress, and I was happy I took it.

The trip to Greece and the surrounding islands was one of the most memorable trips of my life. I was thankful for the opportunity to see Greece and the stunning islands, particularly Santorini and Crete. I owed him for that chance. That first trip was the beginning of many other travels to faraway places. I paid for the other trips but never forgot his kind gesture and his encouragement for me to continue to explore the world.

Tony buoyed my dreams, encouraging me to expand in many ways besides travel. Through the years I learned a lot of things from him. Though shy and soft-spoken, he was bright and charismatic. However, the quality that intrigued me most was his ability to entirely change people's perceptions about him, particularly when they were of a negative nature. I spent years observing his turning vigorous enemies and foes into defending friends. Intrigued, I often asked him how he did it. It was something I wanted to learn. He would shrug and say it was nothing. I was never able to get him to articulate what or how he did it. In time I came to believe it had something to do with his sly sense of humor and self-effacement. Somehow this combination of skills disarmed his adversaries. Whatever his formula was, it always worked. I wasn't funny (though Paul had always maintained I was) or sly, so I was unable to acquire that skill set though I tried.

His dry sense of humor always took me by surprise, and it was another thing I loved about him. When others told him he was funny, he would deny it, saying, "Not really." He didn't see himself that way. Yet, he had a keen eye and had the ability to hone in on humorous events and people effortlessly. He enjoyed laughing and seeing the world through a mirthful window, often chuckling at himself. He lost that spark in his later years as illnesses took their toll on him physically. These were qualities that I envied and wished I possessed. I took myself too seriously and was not always able to see the joyful side of life.

We planned an annual Christmas dinner every year trying to go to a new and fun restaurant. One year he selected a restaurant in the Piedmont area. The plan was that we were to meet there. Dressed up and excited to see him, I arrived early and was dismayed to see the seating arrangements. It was an expensive restaurant; yet they had set up long tables in rows where you sat in close proximity to complete strangers. The maître d' refused to seat me until my other party arrived. I felt concerned about not being able to have any private conversations in such a crowded place. As I stood by the door waiting, he came up and kissed me on the cheek.

"I don't know about this place," I murmured into his ear.

"It will be okay, sweetheart," he said lovingly. "We'll make it work."

"But, Tony, someone might see you and me sitting in these long rows. I don't know if it is a good idea," I muttered. He didn't seem worried so I shouldn't be either; but that was the thing about going out with a married man—an uneasy fear always lurked in the back of my mind.

That particular Christmas dinner stood out whenever I reminisced about our times together. It was a memorable evening filled with luscious food, wine, and an opportunity to share each other's company. It was on these occasions that I sometimes played the "what if we were married" game in my head. I dismissed the idea as soon as it came knowing that it was not to be and in fact was not what I wanted. *Things were fine*, I'd remind myself sternly.

The liaison was a knowing choice. My lover had a loving, close-knit family. He and his wife had committed to remain married even though the relationship had faltered and was strained long before I entered the picture. In my naiveté, I was perfectly content with his staying married. It suited my need for autonomy and to be commitment free.

In my way of thinking this was a suitable compromise. But what about the other woman, some will ask? Yes, after a period of time, Tony's wife learned of my relationship with her husband. At the time I was no threat to her since I did not want to marry him or even have him leave his family. But she was hurt by our long-term affair. How easily self-deception creeps into our defenses!

Our relationship worked for a long time, but then I came to realize I loved him deeply and that his devotion to me distracted him from his commitment to his wife. I'll admit this troubled me; yet I managed to push away any lingering feelings of guilt, blithely ignoring any troubling details that came to the forefront. I continued to rationalize our relationship with such thoughts as that she had most of his time, all his holidays and I had only a couple of hours here and there or sometimes half a day, if it could be managed.

We remained remarkably close over the many years we shared together. Our relationship was not about sex, although there was some in the years before his surgery. It was about intimacy. Intimacy is what most people crave, even more than sex, and that was something he was able to provide. He shared many of the high and low points of my life, holding my hand while I shed tears at disappointments and losses, as well as celebrating my successes. He strongly supported my exposure to a world much larger and more complex than I had come from.

There was no doubt of his love. He confirmed it over and over through the years. The one whose love was more in question was mine. Was I in the relationship to avoid facing my deepest fears about trust? Were all those years about playing it safe? Such thoughts flickered in the back of my mind from time to time, but I dismissed them—too afraid to confront old beliefs head-on. Instead, I remained in a cocooned relationship, oblivious of my own inner rationalizations. If I am now being candid, for me it was about avoiding betrayal at all costs.

Our relationship had its difficulties during the years we were together. We argued often about politics and the direction the world was going. He was older than me and like many, but not all of his generation, believed the world was in general decline and that young people weren't as hard-working as others in his generation had been. "They have it too easy and want everything immediately," he would mutter unhappily. They don't want to wait for anything." I tried to say that his complaint was not true of all the millennials, but my words fell on deaf ears. He was convinced things were getting worse and no one was doing anything about it or even noticing, for that matter.

We spent a great deal of time discussing spiritual things. I was interested in death, how people feel about it and how it is celebrated. I would travel often to Oaxaca or San Miguel de Allende to celebrate the Day of the Dead. I believed death was a transition back to the source where we would see ones we had loved or had met in this life again. Sometimes, I imagined they would join us in our next lifetime for a new play. None of this was appealing to Tony, nor was he a fan of death. He preferred never to discuss it saying he was not going to die in order to end the conversation. Nor was he particularly interested in my ideas about how death and karma worked. He did not buy into any of it. He was clear that dead was dead. We would argue endlessly about reincarnation and about how the world viewed death—mostly by avoidance. We never came to an agreement, and I was sure he was humoring me by even engaging in dialogue on the topic. I regret that we had not planned some type of signal for him to let me know he was all right in the afterlife. I knew he was okay, but would have loved to have a clear sign from him to that effect.

Chapter 31
The Later Years

The later years saw a dramatic increase in Tony's physical problems. First, he had prostate cancer and then started having kidney trouble. His eyesight had always been poor and started to decline more rapidly with age. His gait suffered because of a hip alignment issue. These physical ailments caused him to despair and say it wasn't worth living with these new infirmities. He persevered through, continued working and finally reluctantly retired. Despite physical ailments, Tony still maintained his cheerful stance while minimizing his numerous medical conditions. Finally, his kidneys failed, and he had to go on dialysis. This necessity made his life more difficult, limiting his mobility and visits.

I supported and encouraged him despite his deteriorating health issues. The relationship continued and he would come by my house for a meal, or we would meet at a restaurant near me. Because of the flight of stairs at my house, the restaurant became more convenient for him after a time. It was a place I frequented. It became our new meeting place. Later, when I would return there to eat, the owner whom I knew would ask, "I haven't seen your husband in a while." Rather than say he wasn't my husband, I would simply reply, "He's out of town." After so many years, he felt like a husband.

I tried to be sensitive to how difficult it was for him to get around. He ignored his health disorders as much as he could. He did not like discussing them. It was clear to me they were pulling him down.

On one of my birthday dinners, we celebrated at one of Tony's favorite Mexican restaurants in Berkeley. We favored tables on the second level and even had a favorite seating area. To get a table upstairs, you had to arrive early. It was an upscale restaurant that only served appetizer plates and your bill was determined by the number of plates on your table. That night, we ordered our usual items, enjoying the food tremendously and parting with a brief kiss and a wave.

A month later, Tony called me, extremely upset, saying he had been billed $6,000 for that birthday meal. The credit card company had paid it and he was having trouble getting a refund.

"Didn't you notice the amount when you signed it?" I asked. "No," he ranted. "I couldn't believe they processed a tab for that amount." In his favor, the restaurant was always dark and with his poor vision, he hadn't checked the bill that closely. It took months of haggling to get the restaurant to correct it to $60. He was forced to go to the restaurant's accounting office and argue that it was impossible for two people to create a $6,000 bill in a couple of hours, no matter how much they drank or ate. Fortunately, the bill reflected the number of parties. It would have been more difficult without that information since this restaurant regularly hosted large groups, particularly in the upstairs section we favored. He carefully scrutinized future bills to ensure there would be no more big surprises. On occasion he even asked me to check as he filled in the tip.

Tony always supported me even when we disagreed. Our more serious arguments were often about politics, particularly women in politics. He had a strong dislike for certain well-known female politicians. When I asked him to articulate exactly what it was about them he disliked so intensely, he hemmed and hawed. I secretly believed he didn't like strong, aggressive women, but in a way that didn't make sense because I always heard admiration in his voice when he discussed the strong women he knew. I thought it was fascinating how vociferously he felt about them. I decided it had something to do with strong women who held positions of power. Yes, that was it. Some men are threatened by women with power. Strong women weren't a concern unless they wielded power. When I shared my theory with him, he denied it had any merit.

I remained loyal to Tony throughout the years and was never tempted to have other relationships. I discouraged those who expressed interest.

Chapter 32
The Goodbye Letter

Our lengthy relationship allowed us to share a special intimacy that came with a deep understanding and acceptance of each other. It allowed us to empathize with and accept the other's strengths and weaknesses. We remained remarkably close over the years, so the call from Albert was shocking. He thought he was simply advising me that a former colleague had passed on. He did not know it was a man I had loved for decades and whom I didn't get to say goodbye to when he died. Yes, I had known Tony was slowing down and I worried that he was afraid in his last moments. I prayed that his family had held his hand, reassuring him as he slipped slowly into the next world.

Having missed the opportunity to say goodbye, I knew I had to write Tony a letter expressing my grief and telling him all the things I failed to relay while he was alive. Yet, even after writing the letter I still wanted to share my grief with someone to make it real. With trepidation, I read the letter to my weekly writing group. There was silence when I finished. The members were quick to offer words of support though I could tell they were shocked by my revelations.

Here is the letter I wrote Tony after his death:

My Dearest Tony,

I hadn't heard from you in a while. The last time we spoke you mentioned more medical problems. You promised to call. I have been terribly worried about you.

Albert called today and left a message on my phone. He said you had died the day before. He thought I would be interested since I had worked with you in the past. This news deeply saddened me because I didn't get to say goodbye or even to thank you for your endless kindness. And there is no one with whom I can share my grief about your passing, since you remain a secret, even after all these years.

I looked up your obituary in the East Contra Costa Times. It gave an extensive summary of all your accomplishments, something you always wanted with no naysayers quoted. Your old friends sang your praises as well they should. The article mentioned the park that was not named in your honor while you lived. I bet they'll do it now, but for you it is too late.

What worries me most is that you might have been afraid during your final moments here. I hope your wife or one or both of your daughters were holding your hand in your last moments. You'll recall all the discussions we had about death and how you said you wouldn't die. Even then you did admit you were afraid to die since you didn't know what you believed. You scoffed at my ideas of what happened after death, clearly unconvinced there might be more after we are gone. Even my recycling argument did not influence any change in your thinking.

Was it frightening, Tony? Are you okay? At least your physical ailments are gone, and you've gotten to see your beloved mother and dad. Yes, I know you complained about your mom's tight ways, but I heard the secret admiration in your voice as you spoke of her. And, your quiet shy father, was he there to greet you? Did you notice the newspaper tribute said you were shy also?

There are so many things I want to say to you, Tony, that I should have expressed to you when you were alive. You lived a full life and accomplished much. Looking back, were you happy with your life? Did you have regrets?

I know our relationship was turbulent at times but there was never a doubt of how much you loved me. My friend, Mildred, told me on more than one occasion, "Yollie, that man adores you." Embarrassed, I shrugged off her comments. That was wrong. I know that now.

Looking back, it seems all so long ago. After all, we were together for more than 30 years. So many memories flood my mind. Like the time you went out and bought steaks for a dinner party after I had been fussing about not having enough time to get it all done. The steaks were sitting on the counter as a surprise when I arrived home. Even though you weren't invited you generously went grocery shopping for a frazzled girlfriend.

Then there was the time we were in bed and Albert called and said my daughter had lice and I had to get to his house immediately to take care of the situation. Jumping out of bed and saying I had to go, you called out, "I've been thrown out of bed for many reasons but never for lice before." It's funny now but at the time I was very ashamed and embarrassed.

The clothes and shoes you bought me through the years always brought you so much joy. You are the only man I've known who loved to buy clothes and always with such care and style. Thank you for those lovely items.

We had fun, fights, many fabulous meals, romantic times and so many political arguments. You called yourself an independent, but you had strong convictions about women in politics, which is funny because you loved and respected women, constantly reminding me that we (women) are so much stronger in every way than men. You seemed in awe of all the strong women you had known, including your grandmother and mother.

Dearest, I would be remiss if I failed to express all that I learned from you. I will never forget the day I sat in my office working while co-workers were outside chatting by the coffee machine. They were wasting time instead of working. You strolled into my office and asked why I wasn't outside with the others. Surprised, I said they should be working. You shook your head and said, "Grab your cup and go over there and talk to them." I was outraged, saying I had work to do.

Why was I being chastised when I was the one working? You pointed out that more work can be accomplished by knowing people in your environment and listening to them than sitting in the office. I didn't agree but grabbed my cup reluctantly. How right you were, Tony, and that was such a hard lesson for me but one I learned well. Thanks for forcing me to drink coffee with the others.

The most important lesson you imparted was what to do when I've won a battle, an argument, or a point. To use your exact words, "Yolanda, remove your leg from their neck and back off when you've won. Give them the space to retreat gracefully." For an impatient person who wants to win, this was a hard one. It took me ages to understand how important and how right you were. Sorry about the delay in thanking you for this one.

Oh, Tony, I will deeply miss your sense of humor, your self-deprecating style, your friendship, and your slyness when you thought it wasn't being noticed, but, most of all, your love. I hope you had a safe and worry-free journey. Until we meet again, darling, thanks for lovely memories.

Love,
Yolanda
P.S. Send me a sign (any sign) that you are all right!

Chapter 33
The Later Years with Albert

Albert and I continued to remain in close contact because of our long-term contract and our daughter. The years flew by and yet our relationship remained friendly and loving. I had met and known many of Albert's girlfriends, particularly the long-standing ones. Some were welcoming, some suspicious, and others were threatened by our relationship. Some had difficulty understanding my role in Albert's life. They were unsure why I played such a prominent role in his life after so many years. It made for awkward meetings at celebrations and whenever a new girlfriend showed up.

Albert's second mini-stroke required hospitalization. I was worried about his health. He called me from the hospital requesting a favor. He explained he was dating three women at the same time. This in itself was not at all surprising. What did shock me was that they worked together and none of them was aware of the situation. Albert said they wanted to visit him, and he was afraid they would bump into each other. That would be disastrous. He wanted me to come to the hospital and pretend to be a friend of one of them. It didn't make sense and his request infuriated me. I refused, hung up, and left immediately for the hospital.

Locating his room at the hospital, I marched in, determined to have it out with him. He was dazed to see me after my recent phone call and refusal to assist him.

"Albert," I shouted, "you're 74 years old, for heaven's sake. Make up your damn mind who you want."

"I don't want to live alone any longer," he said sadly.

"Then choose one of them and stop this nonsense!" It was clear to me that he was afraid after his latest medical episode. I actually thought it would do him good to settle down. I was later stunned to learn that when he left the hospital a couple of days later he headed directly to a jewelry shop and bought an engagement ring. He had made his decision. He was going to get married.

He slowly started making wedding plans with his fiancé. I was told the wedding would be a small, intimate event at her home with only immediate family in attendance. I was not invited. This stung because he wouldn't be marrying anyone if I hadn't given him hell at the hospital. Hurt, I pleaded with Albert to let me attend. He said his future wife only wanted immediate family in attendance. I had met his future wife and had a distinct feeling she was uncomfortable with my relationship with Albert. So, I was not totally surprised at not being invited. It was just that I felt I was part of Albert's immediate family and that he should request my presence. The event included Albert's sister, my daughter, and his finance's immediate family.

Noting my peeved response, Albert tried to reassure me by reminding me I was invited to their wedding reception which was being held a couple of months later. This did not appease me, and this was the beginning of a long, tenuous relationship with the new wife. I understood that through the years women close to Albert, girlfriends and lovers, had had difficulty understanding my role in his life. Yes, they knew we had a daughter together, but they did not understand our continued closeness. It had happened so many times with others that I recognized the response and understood how it was mistaken as something more, something threatening.

Amazingly, anyone observing Albert and me together could see how devoted we remained to each other after the earlier years of trials and tribulations. Not as lovers, but as dear friends. Albert would accidentally slip and call me by his wife's name, which did not upset me. He would also unintentionally call his new wife by my name, which did not help to endear her to me.

Eventually, after many years, his wife came to me as the ally that I was, and it was only then that a real friendship developed. We were able to appreciate a man we both loved with no worries or jealousy.

THE SACRED VOW

I observed how lovingly she took care of Albert, and how equally devoted he was to her. He had come a long way from that sad day in the hospital. He was a happily married man and I rejoiced for him. They traveled the world, entertained, enjoyed their wine escapades, and lived happily until his wife became ill. By that time, his wife and I were close friends.

Once his wife's prognosis was revealed as terminal, she worried who would take care of Albert after she was gone. Albert had been the frailer of the two and she had always believed he would die before her; but it was not to be. Before her death, she continued to express concerns about his care. I had told her I would always look after him. At this point Albert and I had been friends for 47 years. For some unknown reason, my words did not seem to please her. So, I stopped reassuring her.

As her time drew near, Albert's wife asked to meet with me. At that time, she handed me the key to her house and said in a loving voice, "You are my rock now." This brought tears to my eyes. I committed to her that I would always watch over Albert. It was a promise I had made long ago and intended to keep. She fought a hard battle for two years before passing away in September 2020.

As the remaining months of 2020 were ending, everyone was repeatedly warned about the dangers of holding family gatherings. COVID was on everyone's mind. Fear reigned high as the medical professionals tried desperately to provide clear information to the public that would reassure them while issuing cautions after cautions about family get-togethers. It would be the first time Albert and I would not have Christmas dinner with our daughter and her family. Albert's wife had passed away a couple of months earlier, so he was all alone. We decided to celebrate Christmas together as we had done repeatedly through the last 38 years. Since it would be just the two of us, we decided to go back to our traditional Christmas dinner of prime rib. It had been years since we had had that meal after others had rebelled against eating red raw meat. We relished the idea of once again eating our favorite Christmas dinner.

As Christmas Eve drew near, I was saddened by the thought we would not be seeing our daughter and her family to celebrate.

I would miss my grandson Santino terribly. Sitting at my brightly decorated table with the candles glowing, I was filled with amazement that Albert and I had once again become principals in each's other lives. It was not something either of us had pondered, even considered, or necessarily wanted; yet by some serendipitously order it had been carefully arranged by the universe. It reminded me of the psychic's prediction of long ago concerning the role Albert would play in my life and the role I would play in his. It was now all coming true. The interesting part was that I no longer harbored angry feelings, misgivings, or a wish for him to disappear. It almost appeared magically orchestrated. The cycle of learning and loving was coming full circle. Hadn't the psychic said, "You will learn to tell each the truth in this lifetime and then you will become good friends?"

How strange, I thought to myself silently. Albert and I are back to where we began – only now as good and loving friends. We toasted each other and the elapsed years and then offered a special toast to his wife.

It was a Christmas I will never forget.

Chapter 34
Final Reflections

In reflection I see why certain paths were not taken, while others were diligently followed. I realize now how fear kept me in one place for an exceptionally long time.

Amazingly, I remained unaware of how deeply imbedded in my life those two particular trajectories were until the actual writing of my memoir. Earlier, I would have been unable to name them or even understand their significance. It was only in retrospect that I could grasp the pattern they weaved in and out my life.

Those continuing themes were the avoidance of betrayal at all costs, and the pursuit of justice and fairness. Both followed me with dogged persistence. Yes, I'll admit the avoidance of betrayal came at a high price, while the quest for making things right, no matter the consequences, served me well in business relationships. The latter was particularly helpful in my younger years as I engaged in an unfamiliar world in which I held no power.

Through the years, family and friends asked me why I didn't marry or at least have a boyfriend. They thought it strange, particularly when I was in my late thirties. When my daughter was young, I said I was waiting until she was older; but the truth was I did have someone. It's just that no one knew about him. Though he knew of the people in my life, he had never met any of them except the two close women friends who knew my secret.

I authored my story to reveal my secret love. So, you can imagine my shock as my words spilled onto the written pages and the real truth hit me—an important truth I had been hiding from myself for a remarkably long time. Writing my story forced me to finally see and acknowledge that I had become a woman so afraid of betrayal that I did not dare or allow myself to risk a commitment—not to the man with whom I'd had a child, or to the one I'd held onto for so many years who had sheltered me from the world I was avoiding. How had I missed it? How had I failed to see what was right in front of me? I had become the very thing I feared most and had spent my entire life trying to avoid—the betrayer not only of the other woman, but ultimately of my own self.

Putting the past in perspective has now freed me to accept what I became and why. And yes, it has helped me forgive myself and for any harm I did to others. That was the hardest part. Telling my story has also made me reconsider which lover left the most lasting imprint on my heart. When I started writing I was certain I knew.

Now I am not so sure.

ACKNOWLEDGEMENTS

I am deeply indebted to all the lovers (the named and the unnamed) who have entered my life for their wisdom and the truths they shared with me. Some did not turn out as I would have liked, but that did not diminish their influence.

I am thankful for the Pinole writing group whose astute ideas always provoke deeper insight and discernment on the story line.

I want to give a special thanks to Emma Arroyave for her initial review and observations before publishing my book.

A special thank you to Karen Mireau for her thoughtful and perceptive comments during the editing process. I appreciate her support as she encouraged me to go deeper into the story.

Finally, I want to thank my daughter Vanessa for her patience in waiting to read my story. I know she was concerned I would divulge some shocking secrets and perhaps I have. Now, sweet daughter, you know all my secrets—well, almost all. I hope you are now reassured that I am human just like all other mothers with my own distinct ideas and imperfections.

www.ingramcontent.com/pod-product-compliance
Lightning Source LLC
Chambersburg PA
CBHW072028110526
44592CB00012B/1436